All the world's a stage,
And all the men and women merely players:
They have their exits and their entrances;
And one man in his time plays many parts …

As You Like It

Shakespeare's plays … Stuffy, convoluted, long-winded? Sure, for some out there. Hence, the purpose of this book – to quickly and painlessly acquaint readers and so-called 'nonreaders' alike with Shakespeare, his world, his words, and his most noteworthy works.

In this day and age, who has the time or patience to pore over long, drawn-out books? Enter this book, its aim being to provide a non-stuffy, non-convoluted, non-long-winded solution, one that lets you become a Shakespeare connoisseur in a fraction of the time it might take your stiflingly snobbish bookworm brother-in-law. Imagine, in 15 minutes flat, being able to be clued in on a play's key plots, characters and commentaries. And suddenly, you've been appointed the office genius!

These condensed, crash-course, water-cooler renderings offer up the highlights of Shakespeare's masterpieces, without all the 'fluff.' A 'Shakespeare at a Glance' chapter includes a brief biography, excerpts from some of his greatest poems, samplings of his rapier wit and level-headed wisdom; a cruelly fun section titled 'Shakespearean Insults: The Art of Name-Calling', unlocks a door into the playwright's psyche by letting you unleash your own playfully biting barbs.

If, as Shakespeare claims, 'all the world's a stage', this volume is your cue to join in on the act.

Contents

Some are born great, some achieve greatness, And some have greatness thrust upon them.

Twelfth Night

SHAKESPEARE AT A GLANCE

COMEDIES
TRAGEDIES
HISTORIES

My words fly up; my thoughts remain below. Words without thoughts never to heaven go.

Hamlet

There's small choice in rotten apples.

… if the while I think on thee, dear friend, All losses are restored, and sorrows end.

In time we hate that which we often fear.

Antony and Cleopatra

... They praise me, and make
an ass of me; now my foes tell me
plainly I am an ass;
so that by my foes, sir, I profit
in the knowledge of myself, and
by my friends I am abused.

Twelfth Night

"Thou marble-hearted insolent noise-maker!"

A Brief Biography:
William Shakespeare, 1564–1616

"Master Poet and Dramatist"

The life of England's foremost dramatic writer is dappled with mystery. In fact, very little is officially "known" about Shakespeare; but scholars have pieced together a reasonably comprehensive picture of his life and passions from traditions, contemporary memoirs, and a lengthy series of records – including his baptism at Stratford-on-Avon in 1564, his marriage to Anne Hathaway in 1582, the christenings of their three children, his patent applications and court testimonies, his lease agreements, tax records and purchase agreements. And most reputable critics irrefutably ascribe to him authorship of the major portion (he likely employed collaborators on some works) of thirty-eight of the world's most respected and ingenious plays, several excellent poems, and some 154 sonnets.

John Shakespeare was a tanner, a dealer in grain, and a Stratford town official. His wife, Mary, was born the daughter of a prosperous gentleman-farmer. When their son William was still a young man, it appears that his father suffered severe financial setbacks. Thus, William must have achieved success largely on his own. He apparently never attended college.

Successive purchases and sales of agricultural products and parcels of land near Stratford must have provided Shakespeare with greatly increased capital, which, when reinvested, paid him a steady income for many years. This gave him the freedom and time to concentrate on his first loves: acting and writing.

Shakespeare the Writer

When Shakespeare began his writing, he was attacked by his fellow playwrights as a "mere actor" presumming to write plays. Then, in 1594–95, he performed before Queen Elizabeth, and his name became widely recognized. Within a few years he was lionized by critics, notably Robert Greene, who compared his "honey-tongued" comedies, tragedies and histories with those of Plautus and Seneca.

In association with Richard Burbage's company of actors, Shakespeare grew in public stature to become one of the owners of London's Globe Theatre in 1599. A decade later, he and his colleagues purchased the enclosed Blackfriars Theatre as a "bad-weather" establishment.

Shakespeare developed a writing style which proved to be both dynamic and one-of-a-kind; a style that incorporated – and transcended – a number of literary elements. He was especially fascinated by the conflict and divergence between *individual feeling* and *public office*. In Shakespeare's plays, what the successful public man might do often seems to go against what the same admirable private man might do, evoking a sustained level of suspense and drama. Additionally, the eventual resolvers of conflict are usually men and women of deep principle, but without the trappings of conventional authority – another line of tension. These two elements can be seen in the character of Hamlet: a private man placed in a public situation (to avenge his father's murder) and asked to act on a matter for which, with his contemplative and peaceful nature, he feels profoundly unfitted.

In harmony with the demands of Elizabethan audiences, Shakespeare laced his plays with twisted plots, allegory, metaphor, puns (even the tragic lovers Romeo and Juliet have a conservative estimate of 175 "quibbles"), word-plays (dual-meanings), and a smooth-tongued, economical use of words.

Even up to the time of his death, on or about his fifty-second birthday in 1616, Shakespeare was still originating distinct, well-turned phrases. His last will and testament and the inscription carved above his tombstone, which lies before the altar of the Stratford church, exemplify this wry style:

Good Friend ... forbear
To dig the dust enclosed here;
Blest be the man that spares these stones
And curst be he who moves my bones.

For study, Shakespeare's works can be divided into six separate, somewhat chronological sections: *Early Works, Major Histories, The Problem Plays, Tragedies, The Roman Plays, and The Late Romances.* His comedies seem to be interspersed throughout these divisions.

Early Works

The historical play was the dominant and most popular form of drama in Shakespeare's day. With his first works, *Henry VI* and *Richard III*, he hammered out his writing methodologies.

In these early works, staging is undeveloped, verse-form is inflexible and sometimes monotonous, and dramatic construction is rather crude. A serious and philosophic tone dominates; imagery and intensity are used over inner conflict to generate drama; no Falstaffian characters arise to add breadth or comic relief. Soliloquies and pauses for self-explanation are common. For instance, *Richard III* begins with a chorus-like introduction ("Now is the winter of our discontent …") and proceeds to describe the general scene before turning to the personal plight of the Machiavellian hero.

These two plays were followed by a prolific number of dramas, comedies and fantasies. *Titus Andronicus, A Midsummer Night's Dream, The Merchant of Venice, The Comedy of Errors, Two Gentlemen of Verona, The Taming of the Shrew* and *Twelfth Night* all come from this period.

Major Histories

Though the popular *Romeo and Juliet* was written during this second period, Shakespeare occupied the majority of his time recording the epic lives of English history – *Richard II, Henry IV,* and the great classic, *Henry V.*

Now the playwright more fully develops his dramatic material to include in-depth examinations of men in high positions, and studies of different personalities reacting to and exercising power. *Richard II* is an ineffective king, unable to properly respond to crisis; Harry of Monmouth, on the other hand, is the prototypical leader of men. In this period, too, plump Falstaff (Henry IV) appears, bringing to the horrors of war and men's pretentiousness his ironic commentary and touch of humanness: "… If to be fat is to be hated, then Pharaoh's lean kine are to be loved …" "Hostess, my breakfast, come! O, I could wish this tavern were my drum." When the comic Falstaff just as suddenly disappears in *Henry V* (he is off-stage, conveniently ill), it evokes an even more horrible sense of villainy and inner fear in the spectators as the onstage portrayals are acted out.

The Problem Plays (Dark Comedies)

"Problem plays," a term coined by F.S. Boas in 1896,
primarily refers to the three plays *Troilus and Cressida*,
All's Well That Ends Well and *Measure for Measure*.
These are commonly considered too serious and analytic
to be classified as comedies, yet they are clearly not
tragedies. They deal with moral concerns, and, depending
on the audience, have been received with both disgust
and applause.

However, *Hamlet* (which was written about the same
time and is usually classified as a tragedy), despite its
many loose ends, has a coherence and dramatic effect
that is missing from the other three. Here the focus is on
Hamlet's predisposition towards reflection rather than
action, which allows us to see man's dilemma – whether to
abide by public codes of conduct or by personal ethics.

Most see these plays as "experiments" that prepare the
way for the great moral questioning and self-discovery that
typify the works which follow.

Tragedies

Othello, Macbeth and *King Lear* highlight the Passionate
Tragedies. In these, Shakespeare transforms melodrama
into tragedy, to explore the forces that destroy men and
empires. The character of Othello – the mirror image of
Hamlet – is unreflective and impulsive; essentially a public

man caught in a domestic situation. When jealousy grips him, his judgment and thinking are clouded, leading to the murder of his wife Desdemona.

The elegant and simple *Macbeth* is a concise and moving account of a man descending into evil. Out of ambition for power springs a masterful and tragic plot. In this play, minor characters, for the first time, take on roles of major moral significance.

In *Lear* we also see poor judgement and blindness to true character. The king ultimately must lose his authority – and his family – in order to capture the vision of how power should rightfully be exercised.

The Roman Plays

The three "Roman" plays all center around human passions and the fall of a great and powerful man. In *Coriolanus, Julius Caesar* and *Antony and Cleopatra*, character relations are illuminated, wonderful speeches delivered, and divided loyalties examined. Note, for example, the contrast between Cassius's invective against Caesar and Brutus's reverence toward Caesar coupled with his undying loyalty to Rome. Here we see opposite values and distinct personalities combining in a common purpose. The plays plunge the audience into politics and treachery (again, both public and private), and, of course, love and death.

The Late Romances

In this last era, Shakespeare may have found himself in a
state of world-weariness. Up to this point he had always
presented at the center of his dramas a great soul in
torment. But in *Cymbeline, The Winter's Tale, Pericles* and
The Tempest, a more magical, unrealistic quality and plot
prevail. These plays depict royal or semi-divine children
recovering their lost beauty or virtue; they celebrate
renewal, forgiveness, beauty and reconciliation, retreating
from politics, power and violence. Shakespeare now uses
more visual and aural effects. This less moving, more
artificial style – possibly designed to help his audiences
see beyond reality to more eternal truths – is seen by some
as a fitting epilogue to the Bard's calculated retreat from
the personal and public tensions of Renaissance life.

Shakespeare's works represent the height of genius.
Many of his famous lines are so well known that they are
even quoted by persons totally unfamiliar with his plays.
His works have profoundly influenced the English
language and its drama for nearly four centuries, and it is
reasonable to assume that his plays – read or viewed – will
continue to provide pleasure and wonderment for
centuries to come.

A Taste of Shakespeare's Poetry

It wasn't until the age of 27 – middle-aged by that era's standards – that Shakespeare began to compose poetry. His often much younger contemporaries, however, agreed that he was the epitome of the master wordsmith. Time has validated that opinion – and even enhanced it.

Many themes are apparent in Shakespeare's poetic body of work; some are lighthearted pieces, some consist of sincere communications, and others contain serious commentary. Yet, in all of the verses there breathes a surplus of power.

This following light verse was apparently written to mock a love sonnet penned by an associate to his fair lady love:

Sonnet CXXX
My mistress' eyes are nothing like the sun;
Coral is far more red than her lips' red:
… I have seen roses demask'd, red and white,
But no such roses see I in her cheeks;
And in some perfumes is there more delight
Than in the breath that from my mistress reeks.
I love to hear her speak, yet well I know

That music hath a far more pleasing sound:
I grant I never saw a goddess go,
My mistress, when she walks, treads on the ground:
And yet, by heaven, I think my love as rare
As any she belied with false compare.

A warning against deceivers is sounded in Shakespeare's earliest-known poem, A Lover's Complaint:

… Further I could say, This man's untrue,
And knew the patterns of his foul beguiling;
Heard where his plants in others' orchards grew
Saw how deceits were gilded in his smiling;
Knew vows were ever brokers to defiling …

Over time, some critics have come to the conclusion that Shakespeare's sonnets are autobiographical in nature, writings through which he could relay his perceptions and experiences. Other critics assert that the poems are mere figments of their author's fertile imagination.

The first 126 sonnets are dedicated to a young friend of Shakespeare's, while the remaining 28 appear to be written to a "dark lady" who steals both his own heart and that of his young friend. The poet imagines that the Dark Lady holds some sort of strange power over him, but he feels helpless to do anything about it, as is revealed in the first stanza of Sonnet CXLVII:

My love is as a fever, longing still
For that which longer nurseth the disease;
Feeding on that which doth preserve the ill,
The uncertain sickly appetite to please …

Shakespeare understood the power of time – in the world and in the lives of people. The words, meter and rhyme all work together in this sonnet to accomplish his purpose:

Sonnet LXIV
When I have seen by Time's fell hand defaced
The rich-proud cost of outworn buried age;
When sometime lofty towers I see down-razed,
And brass eternal, slave to mortal rage;
When I have seen the hungry ocean gain
Advantage on the kingdom of the shore,
And the firm soil win of the watery main,
Increasing store with loss, and loss with store;
When I have seen such interchange of state,
Or state itself confounded to decay;
Ruin hath taught me thus to ruminate –
That Time will come and take my love away.
This thought is as a death, which cannot choose
But weep to have that which it fears to lose.

As powerful as time is, the poet obviously believes that love can persist through time.

Sonnet XXX

When to the sessions of sweet silent thought
I summon up remembrance of things past,
I sigh the lack of many a thing I sought,
And with old woes new wail my dear times' waste:
Then can I drown an eye, unused to flow,
For precious friends hid in death's dateless night.
And weep afresh love's long-since cancell'd woe,
And moan the expense of many a vanish'd sight.
Then can I grieve at grievances foregone,
And heavily from woe to woe tell o'er
The sad account of fore-bemoaned moan,
Which I new pay as if not paid before.
But if the while I think on thee, dear friend,
All losses are restored, and sorrows end.

Other sonnets speak of the power of love to outlast time.
One is among the most popular:

Sonnet CXVI

Let me not to the marriage of true minds
Admit impediments. Love is not love
Which alters when it alteration finds,
Or bends with the remover to remove:
O no; it is an ever-fixed mark,
That looks on tempest, and is never shaken;
It is the star to every wandering bark,
Whose worth's unknown, although his height be taken.

Love's not Time's fool, though rosy lips and cheeks
Within his bending sickle's compass come;
Love alters not with his brief hours and weeks,
But bears it out even to the edge of doom.
If this be error, and upon me proved,
I never writ, nor no man ever loved.

Occasional despair flows through the sonnets. Shakespeare
mourns disappointments, dissatisfactions, losses, the
death of friends. Yet in each case, before the piece ends,
his beloved Dark Lady reassures him and rejuvenates him.
And for a time, a new theme emerges: not only does love
conquer time, it conquers all.

Sonnet XXIX

When in disgrace with fortune and men's eyes,
I all alone beweep my outcast state,
And trouble deaf Heaven with my bootless cries,
And look upon myself, and curse my fate,
Wishing me like to one more rich in hope,
Featured like him, like him with friends possessed,
Desiring this man's art, and that man's scope,
With what I most enjoy contented least;
Yet in these thoughts myself almost despising,
Haply I think on thee – and then my state
(Like the lark at break of day arising
From sullen earth) sings hymns at heaven's gate;

For thy sweet love remember'd such wealth brings,
That then I scorn to change my state with kings.

Shakespeare's lengthy The Rape of Lucrece is based on a
historical tale of a Roman emperor's son, Tarquin, who
is entranced by the great virtue of a married noblewoman,
Lucrece. Unable to assail that virtue, he finally resorts
to raping his paradigm. Afterward, as she mourns the act,
we hear yet another description of the power of time:

Time's glory is to calm contending kings,
To unmask falsehood, and bring truth to light,
To stamp the seal of time in aged things,
To wake the morn, and sentinel the night,
To wrong the wronger till he render right;
    To ruinate proud buildings with thy hours
    And smear with dust their glitt'ring tow'rs …
O, this dread night, wouldst thou one hour come back,
I could prevent this storm, and shun thy wrack!

Shakespeare's plays frequently portray how mankind's
carnal appetites and lust for power or position lead to fatal
mistakes that destroy lives. In his poetry, these same deadly
motivations are in force, as in Lucrece's thorough
assessment of Tarquin's actions:

So that in venturing ill we leave to be
The things we are, for that which we expect;
And this ambitious foul infirmity,
In having much, torments us with defect
Of that we have: so then we do neglect
The thing we have, and, all for want of wit,
Make something nothing, by augmenting it.

The reader can feel the woman's terror as she describes trying to save herself by reasoning with an unreasonable man:

She conjures him by high almighty Jove,
By knighthood, gentry, and sweet friendship's oath,
By her untimely tears, her husband's love,
By holy human law, and common troth,
By heaven and earth, and all the power of both,
   That to his borrow'd bed he make retire,
   And stoop to honour, not to foul desire....
'My husband is thy friend, for his sake spare me;
Thyself are mighty, for thine own sake leave me;
Myself a weakling, do not then ensnare me;
Thou look'st not like deceit, do not deceive me;
My sighs, like whirlwinds, labour hence to heave thee.
   If ever man were moved with woman's moans,
   Be moved with my tears, my sighs, my groans.

Alas, the story comes to a tragic end. Lucrece, having called upon an assembly of gallant knights to defend her honor, names her tormentor, then unsheathes a knife and takes her own life. Her father, and then her husband, come upon the dreadful scene and lament Lucrece's loss.

At last, noble Brutus enters and rebukes the two grieving men; woe is not a proper "cure" for woe, he chides. Rather, they must seek revenge on the vile Tarquin. Moved by these words, the men reply:

Her wrongs to us, and by this bloody knife,/We will revenge the death of this true wife.

The final seven lines, then, read like the final act of one of the Bard's most gripping plays:

When they had sworn to this advised doom,
They did conclude to bear dead Lucerce thence;
To show her bleeding body thorough Rome,
And so to publish Tarquin's foul offence:
Which being done with speedy diligence,
The Romans plausibly did give consent
To Tarquin's everlasting banishment.

Wit and Wisdom in Shakespeare

Some are born great, some achieve greatness,
and some have greatness thrust upon them.
Twelfth Night

Wisely, and slow. They stumble that run fast.
Romeo and Juliet

Ambition should be made of sterner stuff.
Julius Caesar

Some griefs are medicinal.

What's gone and what's past help
Should be past grief.
The Winter's Tale

What's done is done.
Macbeth

Costly thy habit as thy purse can buy,
But not express'd in fancy; rich, not gaudy;
For the apparel oft proclaims the man.
Hamlet

Doubt is a thief that often makes us fear to tread where
we might have won.

Paraphrased version of Shakespeare's Measure for Measure

Nothing can come of nothing.

King Lear

Some are born great, some achieve greatness,
and some have greatness thrust upon them.

Twelfth Night

Upon what meat doth this our Caesar feed,
That he is grown so great?

Julius Caesar

… Our doubts are traitors, and make us lose the good
we oft might win by fearing to attempt.

Measure for Measure

Oh, how bitter a thing it is to look into happiness
through another man's eyes.

When to the sessions of sweet silent thought
I summon up remembrance of things past,
I sigh the lack of many a thing I sought,
And with old woes new wail my dear time's waste.

Ignorance is the curse of God,
Knowledge the wing wherewith we fly to heaven.
Henry VI

My words fly up; my thoughts remain below.
Words without thoughts never to heaven go.
Hamlet

All the world's a stage,
And all the men and women merely players:
They have their exits and their entrances;
And one man in his time plays many parts …
As You Like It

It is a wise father that knows his own child.
The Merchant of Venice

Life every man holds dear;
but the dear man holds honor far more precious
– dearer than life.

Mine honor is my life; both grow in one;
Take honor from me and my life is done.

Neither a borrower nor a lender be.
Hamlet

Small things make base men proud.

This above all: to thine own self be true,
And it must follow, as the night the day,
Thou canst not then be false to any man.
Hamlet

To business that we love we rise betime.
And go to't with delight.
Antony and Cleopatra

Are these things, then, necessities?
Then let us meet them like necessities.
King Henry IV

Weariness
Can snore upon the flint, when resty sloth
Finds the down pillow hard.

Children wish fathers looked but with their eyes;
fathers that children with their judgment looked;
and either may be wrong.

Had I a dozen sons – each in my love alike …
I had rather have eleven die nobly for their
country
than one voluptuously surfeit out of action.

It is not in the stars to hold our destiny but in
ourselves;
we are underlings.

I do love my country's good with a respect more tender,
more holy and profound, than mine own life.

The first thing we do, let's kill all the lawyers.
King Henry VI

They say, best men are molded out of faults; and for the
most become much more better for being a little bad.
Measure for Measure

A politician [is] one that would circumvent God.

It is not strange that even our loves should change with
our fortunes.

When fates impose, that men must needs abide;
It boots not to resist both wind and tide.

The lunatic, the lover and the poet
Are of imagination all compact.
Such tricks hath strong imagination,
That if it would be but apprehend some joy,

This is a gift that I have, a foolish extravagant spirit,
full of forms, figures, shapes, objects, ideas, apprehensions,
motions, revolutions, these are begot in the ventricle of
memory, nourished in the womb … and delivered upon
the mellowing of occasion.

It comprehends some bringer of that joy;
Or in the night, imagining some fear,
How easy is a bush supposed a bear!

There's small choice in rotten apples.
In time we hate that which we often fear.
Antony and Cleopatra

I have had a dream, past the wit of man to say what dream
it was.

Men at some time are masters of their fates.

The world is still deceiv'd with ornament …
In religion, what damned error but some sober brow will
bless it, and approve it with a text, hiding the grossness
with fair ornament? There is novice so simple but assumes
some mark of virtue on his outward parts. How many
cowards, whose hearts are all as false as stairs of sand, wear
yet upon their chins the beards of Hercules and frowning
Mars; who inward searched, have livers white as milk?
The Merchant of Venice

Thou shalt have justice, more than thou desir'st.
The Merchant of Venice

… They praise me, and make an ass of me; now my foes
tell me plainly I am an ass; so that by my foes, sir, I profit in
the knowledge of myself, and by my friends I am abused.
Twelfth Night

And often times excusing a fault doth make the fault worse
by excuse, – as patches set upon a little breach discredit
more in hiding of the fault than did the fault before it was
so patched.
King John

Lord, what fools these mortals be!

What a piece of work is man, how noble in reason, how
infinite in faculty, in form and moving how like an angel,
in appearance HOW LIKE A GOD.

Oh, call back yesterday, bid time return.
Richard II

We are such stuff
As dreams are made on,
and our little life
Is rounded with a sleep.

Shakespearean Insults

The Art of Name-Calling

Shakespeare, noted for creating new words from old, new nouns from common verbs, is even better known for the witty one-liner, the acerbic put-down, the caustic retort. You, too, can get in on the act, so to speak, creating your own Shakespearean insults. Using some of the Bard's more biting words and phrases, found in two lists on the following page, your taunts may be suitable – or not – for the office, amongst friends, or whilst on the road. In the interest of good taste, some of the playwright's more bawdy barbs, slights and expletives have been avoided, while maintaining the pungent, playfully biting, acid-tongued quality of his words.

Create a tart insult by beginning with "You ..." or, better yet, "Thou ..." – then let the words flow, stringing together one or two fitting adjectives from the first list and ending with a well-chosen noun (or adjective-noun combination) from the second list. An example would be: "Thou foul, pestilent, viperous worm!"

Turn the page to play ...

Opening Adjectives

Abominable	Lousy
Bald-pated	Marble-hearted
Barren-spirited	Meddling
Base-born	Milk-livered
Beef-witted	Misshapen
Beetle-headed	Most degenerate
Bloodthirsty	Most foul
Blunt-witted	Most senseless
Brainsick	Most untoward
Brazen-faced	Motley-minded
Brutish	Muddy-mottled
Cank'red	Mumbling
Clay-brained	Naughty
Crooked-pated	Outward-sainted
Damned	Pernicious
Degenerate	Pestilent
Dunghill	Prating
Effeminate	Rump-fed
Fat-brained	Scurvy
Fat-kidneyed	Servile
Flap-eared	Shag-haired
Foul	Shameless
Foul-mouthed	Shrill-voiced
Graceless	Slovenly
Greasy	Small-knowing
Hag-born	Sour
Half-face	Stoney-hearted
Hare-brained	Ugly
Heartless	Unpolish'd
Heedless	Unwholesome
Hell-bound	Venomous
High-minded	Wasp-stung
Hollow-eyed	Whining
Homely	
Idle-headed	
Ill-favored	
Impudent	
Knot-pated	
Lecherous	
Lily-livered	
Logger-headed	

Ending Nouns / Adjective-Nouns

babbling gossip	dreadful
baboon	minister of hell
bag of flax	dull thing
baggage	dull-eyed
base newsmonger	fool
basilisk	dunghill
bean-fed	dunghill
horse	dwarf
bloodsucker	embossed
boil	carbuncle
boor	false hound
braggart	fellow o' th'
braggart vile	strangest mind
brazen-face	i' th' world
breeder of dire	filthy piece of
events	work
burly-boned	fishmonger
clown	flibbertigibbet
canker blossom	fool, that has no
child of hell	more brain
cloakbag of guts	than a stone
clod	foolish gnat
clownish fool	foul blot
commonest	foul defacer of
creature	God's
counterfeit rascal	handiwork
cream-fac'd loon	foul indigested
creeping	lump
venomed thing	foul swine
crusty botch of	foul wrinkled
nature	witch
cut-throat dog	freckled whelp
detested parasite	gnat
devil incarnate	gravel heart
dilatory sloth	greasy tallow-
disease	catch
dissentious rogue	green-sickness
dog-ape	carrion
dolt	hag of hell
double-dealer	hag-seed
doughy youth	half-lunatic

half-penny
purse of wit
harbinger of
blood and death
heir of shame
hellhound
hodge-pudding
idol of idiot-
worshippers
illiterate loiter
incontinent varlet
insolent noise-
maker
intolerable
entrails
issue of a mangy
dog
jolt-head
lack-brain
lack-love
lean-witted fool
leprous witch
loathsome leper
loathsomest scab
loggerhead
louse
louse of a lazar
lout
lump of foul
deformity
lunatic
mad soul
mad wag
mad-brain
madcap
mad-cap ruffian
maggot-pie
malt-horse
drudge
maltworm
mannish coward

marble-breasted
tyrant
mildewed ear
milksop
minimus
minnow of mirth
miscreant
miserable
wretch
mongrel
monster of
ingratitude
monstrous
malefactor
most profane
coxcomb
mountain-goat
mouse of virtue
mouse-eaten dry
cheese
nag
night-brawler
nit
noisome stench
odiferous stench
old goat
one light of brain
one not worth
a gooseberry
parasite
parcel of dropsies
peevish brat
peevish fool
peevish schoolboy
piece of valiant
dust
pigeon-liver
plague-sore
poisonous bunch-
backed toad
polecat

popinjay
prince of fiends
progeny of evils
promise-breaker
puke-stocking
punk
quintessence of
dust
rag
rag-of-muffin
rascally knave
rat without a tail
rat-catcher
red-tailed
bumble-bee
roastmeat for
worms
rooting hog
rotten apple
rotten medlar
rotten thing
salt-butter rogue
sanctimonious
pirate
saucy lackey
scarecrow
scolding
crookback
screech-owl
scurvy lord
serpent heart
serpent's egg
she-wolf
shoulder-clapper
slander of thy
heavy mother's
womb
slug
so vile a lout
son of darkness
soulless villain

sourest-natured
dog
spendthrift of
tongue
sponge
spotted snake
sweet sewer
testy babe
thing most
brutish
thorny
hedgehog
ticklebrain
toadstool
toothpicker
troubler of the
world's peace
turd
valiant flea
varlet vile
very dull fool
very scurvy
fellow
very toad
vile one
viperous worm
wagtail
want-wit
wench
wife of small wit
withered hag
worm
worm's meat
writhled shrimp
young up-start

The actors stumbled and botched the performance so completely that the tragedy became comedy ...

A Midsummer Night's Dream

Shakespeare at a Glance

Comedies

Tragedies

Histories

"I to the world am like
a drop of water
That in the ocean seeks
another drop;
Who, falling there to
find his fellow forth,
Unseen, inquisitive,
confounds himself ..."

The Comedy of Errors

All that glitters is not gold

The Merchant of Venice

… Love all, trust a few,
Do wrong to none …

All's Well That Ends Well

"There is a merry war betwixt Signior Benedick and her …" Leonato noted. "A skirmish of wits between them."

Much Ado About Nothing

They had managed to rescue several bottles of liquor from the ship and were lumbering about on the sand, blind drunk …

The Tempest

The Taming of the Shrew

TYPE OF WORK

Dramatic, farcical comedy

SETTING

Warwickshire, England,
and Padua, Italy;
Sixteenth century

PRINCIPAL CHARACTERS

Christopher Sly
An indolent, fat tinker

Baptista Minola
A rich Italian gentleman

Bianca
His refined, youngest daughter

Katherine
His sharp-tongued, eldest daughter

Gremio
Bianca's rich and elderly suitor

Hortensio
Bianca's other suitor

Petruchio
Hortensio's friend

Lucentio
A rich and colorful gentleman

Tranio
Lucentio's servant

The hostess of the inn bellowed at the drunken tinker, berating him for the glasses he had burst and threatening to call the constable. "Let him come," mumbled Christopher Sly as he slid under a stool and began to snore. The hostess shook her fist and ran out. At that moment, in strode a gallantly plumed lord with his servants.

The lord was a mischievous sort, and he, deciding that it would be an excellent joke to change this swinish drunkard slumped at his feet into a lord, ordered his servants to drag the man to his mansion, wash him, dress him in fine apparel, and lay him in the richest chamber. The company set off to do their lord's bidding.

Christopher Sly awoke. He blinked in the light of the magnificent room in which he found himself. He was sitting on a mountain of cushions; servants bowed to him in honor. Thinking this must all be the work of strong drink – as was often the case – he cried for more ale. When he was served all manner of rich food and drink, he objected, complaining that he was a simple tinker unaccustomed to such fare. As their lord had instructed them, the servants then informed him that Christopher Sly the tinker did not exist; that he was indeed a lord who had awakened from a bad dream.

Next, accompanied by sultry music, in danced the new lord's "wife," in fact a pageboy dressed in the fine raiment of a lady. Straightway, the tinker-lord wanted to carry her off to bed; but the servants insisted he must guard his strength, for he had been ill many weeks. So the ardent husband was forced to sit modestly by his bride and watch a play.

As he looked on, he became transfixed by the dream-like drama that unfolded before his eyes:

In Padua, an old Italian town, lived rich old Baptista Minola and his two daughters. The younger girl, Bianca, was an angel from heaven; the elder, Katherine, was a scourge from the "other place," with a mustard-hot temper and a sizzling tongue to match. Katherine had no suitors, while Bianca had two, which posed a problem for their father. Baptista would not allow the younger Bianca to marry unless someone took Katherine off his hands first – but surely it would "snow in hell" before any man married such a shrew!

Baptista pled with Bianca's two suitors, elderly moneybag, Gremio and the younger Hortensio, to consider, instead, his eldest daughter. They vigorously shook their heads. The resigned father then charged them to find a tutor for his cherished young Bianca and hurried into the house, leaving the hapless pair to the mercies of Katherine. They soon conceded that if either wished to woo gentle Bianca, they must find a husband for her scolding sister.

Two strangers from Pisa had witnessed this family scene. One, Lucentio, had fallen in love with Bianca at first glimpse, and he caught upon the idea of becoming her tutor. When his servant Tranio reminded him that he had business errands in Padua for his father, Lucentio convinced Tranio to trade places with him. He would be two places at once – on business in the name of Lucentio,

> … surely it would "snow in hell" before any man married such a shrew!

and as tutor-lover in the name of Tranio. The two exchanged clothes, and Lucentio stood transformed into a humble schoolteacher, while Tranio, in his master's wonderful raiment, became a wealthy merchant.

Meanwhile, Hortensio, still pondering possible ploys to marry off Katherine, encountered an old friend from Verona, Petruchio, who expressed a desire "to wive it wealthily in Padua." Hortensio impulsively alluded to Katherine, but then squelched the idea; he could not wish such a woman on his friend. But, amazingly, the thought of a spirited heiress was to Petruchio's liking, and Hortensio at last agreed to help him meet Katherine. In return, he asked Petruchio to recommend a schoolmaster for Bianca – who would, of course, be Hortensio himself, in disguise.

Then came Gremio, with a schoolmaster of his own to present to Baptista – the starry-eyed Lucentio. Behind

… accompanied by sultry music, in danced the new lord's "wife," in fact a pageboy dressed in the fine raiment of a lady.

them sauntered colorful Tranio, also on his devious way to woo Bianca – in his master's name.

As the beaus lined up to vie for Bianca's love, each agreed to pay an allotted amount to Petruchio for removing the impediment – Katherine – that blocked their contest for her lovely younger sister. Petruchio, money in his pocket, beamed with joy.

Baptista had just reprimanded Katherine for her abusive manners, when visitors arrived. He was pleased that Gremio had found a suitable schoolmaster to teach Bianca in Latin and Greek, and even more pleased that a fine-looking, courteous gentleman, Petruchio of Verona, was inquiring after Katherine. "Pray have you not a daughter called Katherina, fair and virtuous?"

"I have a daughter called Katherina," Baptista responded, leaving it at that.

Petruchio, too, had brought a "learned" schoolmaster to teach Bianca in musical skills. And then still another suitor appeared to seek Bianca's hand – a colorful, richly dressed young "gentleman" from Pisa. What a glorious day! The father had secured, in a matter of minutes,

… if either wished to woo gentle Bianca, they must find a husband for her scolding sister.

Katherine, was a scourge … with a mustard-hot temper and a sizzling tongue to match.

a suitor for each of his daughters, and two schoolmasters. He turned quickly to Petruchio to settle on the amount of the dowry before the young fellow could change his mind.

When Petruchio finally did meet Katherine, he was genuinely taken with her, and began to court her amid a battle of wit and wills. She frowned; he smiled. She called him an ass; he called her a woman. Still, passion would not be deterred, for truly she was a beauty – though a sour one. When Katherine railed to her father about her hatred for her suitor, Petruchio, with utmost cheerfulness, assured Baptista that all was well; in fact, he would soon be off to Venice to purchase wedding clothes. "Kiss me, Kate!" he cried, seizing her around the waist. "We will be married o' Sunday!"

Baptista, meanwhile, decided to betroth his popular Bianca to the highest bidder. Rich Gremio gleefully began to offer more and more of his properties, but each offer was bested by Tranio. Finally Gremio could offer nothing else and it appeared that Tranio had won Bianca.

All this time, Lucentio had been "tutoring" Bianca, not in Latin, but in love. He had confessed that he had disguised himself to make love to her, and that his servant Tranio was at that moment seeking, under Lucentio's name, to win her hand from her father.

Hortensio also sought a chance to teach Bianca in love, rather than music. But Bianca would have none of the man, proclaiming the Latinist as her choice.

The afternoon arrived for Kate's wedding to Petruchio. As part of a campaign to tame his wild bride, the groom showed up late, wearing rags and odd boots, and carrying a broken sword. In a drunken state, he cuffed the sexton and kissed Katherine with an "echoing smack" that could

> She frowned; he smiled. She called him an ass; he called her a woman.

be heard throughout the church. At the wedding feast, he grabbed Katherine and, waving his battered sword, whisked her out of the hall to his shabby house. Baptista, more afraid *of* his daughter than *for* her, could only mutter, "Nay, let them go; a couple of quiet ones."

By now, Hortensio, tired of watching Bianca swoon so unaccountably over the pathetic Tranio, had decided to turn his attentions to a wealthy and eager Paduan widow. But first he would see how his friend Petruchio had fared with the mean-spirited Kate.

Hortensio found Kate much changed – and miserable. Each time Petruchio's servants offered Kate food, her husband had contemptuously rejected it as unworthy of her. A tailor had brought her fine linen gowns, but Petruchio found fault in everything. Finally, he ordered the aching, weary woman onto a horse, and they both started back to Baptista's mansion. Petruchio had broken Katherine's will. This plain, rough fellow had weathered her storms and thrown them back in her face.

"Pray have you not a daughter called Katherina, fair and virtuous?"
"I have a daughter called Katherina."

A wedding feast of huge proportions was soon held in old Baptista's house. A triple marriage was celebrated: Lucentio, at last as himself, had gained Baptista's blessing to wed Bianca; Hortensio had briskly courted his "ripe plum" of a widow; and Kate and Petruchio were now heart-to-heart in love.

At the wedding feast, Katherine's father drunkenly consoled Petruchio, saying, "I think thou hast the veriest shrew of all." But Petruchio disagreed, and wagered a hundred dollars that his Kate would obey his command to come to him more quickly than the other two brides would come at their husbands' calls; Kate by now surpassed the others in courtesy and attention to duty. When the three wives were summoned, only Kate appeared. In a seemingly demeaning gesture, she knelt and placed her hand beneath her husband's foot. But the act had not brought her down; it had raised her husband up, and showed to the silent guests how much she esteemed Petruchio. "Why, there's a wench! Come on, and kiss me, Kate!" he roared. He had courted her out of love of coins, but now he knew no greater riches than the coins of love.

He had courted her out of love of coins, but now he knew no greater riches than the coins of love.

Night fell. With Petruchio and Kate gone to bed, the empty chamber was silent – except for the soft snoring of a tinker, asleep on the floor.

COMMENTARY

This rough and bawdy play-within-a-play is unlike most of Shakespeare's works. Instead of lyrical poetry and delicate humor, *The Taming of the Shrew* is filled with coarse, vivid puns. In fact, some claim this disparity as evidence that Shakespeare was not the play's sole author.

Nonetheless, it is one of The Bard's most popular works. The lusty main characters have become models for the shrewish woman and the strong-willed woman-tamer.

The Tempest

TYPE OF WORK

Romantic fantasy

SETTING

A remote island;
Fifteenth century

PRINCIPAL CHARACTERS

Prospero
*The rightful Duke of Milan,
castaway on an island in the sea*

Miranda
His beautiful daughter

Alonso
King of Naples

Ferdinand
Alonso's son

Antonio
*Prospero's wicked brother, and false
Duke of Milan*

Sebastian
Alonso's brother

Gonzalo
A kind philosopher

Trinculo and Stephano
Two drunken courtiers

Ariel
Prospero's spirit servant

Caliban
Prospero's grotesque slave-monster

A great tempest arose that drove a certain ship, bound to Naples from Tunis, off its course and onto an uncharted island. The storm had been magically called up by Prospero, one of the two human inhabitants of the island, in order to bring the vessel to shore.

P rospero had once been the mighty Duke of Milan, and had reigned justly. But he had grown so absorbed in his intellectual pursuits – most of them relating to the supernatural – that he turned over the tedious reins of government to his "trusted" brother Antonio, freeing himself to devote his time to the library and the studies he loved. But, sadly, his ambitious brother, taking advantage of Prospero's naiveté, usurped his power – a plan he was only able to carry out with the help of Alonso, the King of Naples and sworn enemy of Milan. Antonio and Alonso cruelly captured Prospero and his infant daughter Miranda, and set them adrift at sea in a small, rotting craft. They would have been drowned – Antonio's wish – had not a counselor on the ship, Gonzalo, provided them with food and drink, and with those volumes from Prospero's collection that contained his magic spells.

... he turned over the tedious reins of government to his "trusted" brother ... But sadly, his ambitious brother, taking advantage of Prospero's naivete, usurped his power.

When Prospero and Miranda washed ashore on their remote island, they found two rather unusual inhabitants. The first was a fairy spirit named Ariel, who had been imprisoned within a tree by her former master, a witch named Sycorax. Prospero freed Ariel from the tree and thus became her new master.

The other creature, Caliban, son of Sycorax, was a lumbering, deformed, half-savage figure. He hated Prospero – and everyone and everything else, for that matter – but was also forced to acknowledge him as master. For twelve years Prospero had kindly ruled over the other three islanders, all the while practicing a form of benevolent sorcery.

Why, then, did Prospero incite the elements to cause this ship to be tossed aground on his island? Because he knew, as it turned out, that the ship bore the very people who had usurped him of his power so many years before – Antonio, Alonso, and their courtiers. The kind, wise Gonzalo was also aboard, along with Ferdinand, Alonso's honorable son. Prospero's plan was to magically scatter

… by killing your brother Alonso as he sleeps, you could become King of Naples.

the passengers about the island in three groups, put them
through a series of trials and adventures by which the
bad would be chastised and the good rewarded, and then
bring them all together to make peace once and for all.

Alonso, together with Antonio, Sebastian, Gonzalo,
and others, found themselves together on the beach.
They were astonished to discover that not only had they
survived the shipwreck, but that their clothes were clean,
dry and pressed (one of Prospero's many bits of magic).
However, Alonso did not see Ferdinand among the
survivors, and supposing his son had drowned, cried out
in grief. Still the good-hearted counselor, old Gonzalo
tried to cheer the distraught Alonso, but Sebastian joined
Antonio in mocking his efforts at optimism.

At this time, the invisible Ariel came on the scene.
By playing her lilting music she caused a deep sleep to
come upon everyone except Sebastian and Antonio.
The situation prompted Antonio to tempt Sebastian with
a proposition: "My strong imagination sees a crown
dropping upon thy head," he began. He went on to say,
in effect, "You remember how simple it was for me to seize
the entire rule of Milan by overthrowing my brother?
Well, by killing your brother Alonso as he sleeps, you could
become King of Naples. No one would ever know how
you ascended to the throne." Sebastian succumbed to the
temptation, and was just about to strike off his brother's
head when Ariel awakened the company. Antonio's plot
had been frustrated.

As the men tramped awkwardly around the island in
hopes of finding Ferdinand alive, Sebastian and Antonio
looked forward to a second opportunity to murder Alonso.
But suddenly the group was beset by a miraculous vision,
sent by Prospero: a numerous troupe of fairies and sprites,

dancing about a table laden with rich foods. The hungry company, invited to eat, was just about to partake, when suddenly lightning struck and thunder rolled; Ariel appeared in the form of a Harpy (a greedy monster, part woman and part bird). As quickly as it had appeared, |the banquet table vanished. Then Ariel rebuked Alonso, Antonio and Sebastian for the crimes they had committed – or had intended to commit – and led them all, guilt-stricken and humbled, to Prospero.

No sooner had Ferdinand set eyes on Prospero's unspoiled, tenderhearted daughter, than he fell in love with her, and she with him.

Ferdinand had landed on another part of the island. As he mourned the father he believed to have drowned, he found himself helplessly guided by Ariel's music to Prospero and Miranda. No sooner had Ferdinand set eyes on Prospero's unspoiled, tenderhearted daughter, than he fell in love with her, and she with him. Prospero, however, concealed his pleasure in seeing these two youngsters so much enthralled by one another, and refused to allow Ferdinand to take Miranda as his queen until he had undergone an ordeal to prove his devotion. The wise magician then ordered the young prince to spend the day lugging and stacking a pile of huge logs, menial labor unbefitting royalty. But Ferdinand gladly accepted the task. He toiled, even through the pleadings of his beloved: "… Pray you, work not so hard! My father is hard at study. He's safe for these three hours."

Now Prospero was indeed at study; not the study of books, but of hearts. As he watched the two lovers, he smiled at his innocent daughter's conspiracy, and sighed with joy at Ferdinand's refusal to slacken his work.

When Prospero was satisfied with Ferdinand's probation, he gave him Miranda's hand and instructed the pair to wait with him until the other castaways should arrive.

Stephano and Trinculo, one a butler and the other a jester, had turned up on still another stretch of the island. They had managed to rescue several bottles of liquor from the ship and were lumbering about on the sand, blind drunk, when they had the misfortune of bumping into hideous Caliban, lying on the beach under a stinking cloak. After accepting a drink from the staggering courtiers, Caliban, now tipsy himself, promised to help them obtain sovereignty over the island – if they would help him murder the present ruler, Prospero. The drunkards agreed, and the three set off in a comical daze to seek out the magician. Ariel overheard their conspiracy and intervened to thwart their plan by placing diversions in their path – attacking hounds; rich, tempting raiment dangling on elusive clotheslines; and many other such conjurations.

Later, Ariel drove the pathetic trio through filthy ditches, swamps, and brier patches, until they finally reached Prospero's cave.

Now, with the entire ship's population reunited – minus Ferdinand, who was playing chess with Miranda inside

Now Prospero was indeed at study; not the study of books, but of hearts.

Prospero gathered everyone into an enchanted circle and revealed his true identity.

the cave – Prospero gathered everyone into an enchanted circle and revealed his true identity. All were astonished, as they had thought the duke was long dead. Prospero mildly rebuked all the schemers of evil: First Alonso and Antonio, for overthrowing his dukedom and leaving him to perish; then Sebastian, for plotting to kill Alonso; and lastly Trinculo and Stephano, for conniving with Caliban to murder him. Then, assured that the company had repented of their evil deeds and intentions, he granted his full, sovereign forgiveness to all.

Prospero next warmly commended his benefactor Gonzalo for his "saintly" character and behavior. Finally, he beckoned penitent Alonso to enter the cave. There, the father tearfully embraced the son he had thought dead. When introduced to Miranda, Ferdinand's cherished bride-to-be, Alonso was equally captivated by her.

… assured that the company had repented of their evil deeds and intentions, he granted his full, sovereign forgiveness to all.

And now, with joy and reconciliation reigning, Ariel reported to Prospero that the beached vessel was repaired and ready for a return voyage to Milan. Before departing the island, however, the old magician, in a final act of kindness, freed Ariel from her servitude. He then took his books and staff and cast them into the sea, openly vowing to give up his long-held practice of sorcery.

Prospero sailed with the company back to Italy – to begin life anew, to reign once more in Milan, and to witness the marriage of his daughter to faithful Ferdinand.

COMMENTARY

This unusual play – full of music, magic, conspiracy, romance, comedy, and pathos – belongs to the last period of Shakespeare's career. The odd, bittersweet drama embodies qualities of both tragedy and comedy, though this and others of the final plays are usually classified as "romances."

In *The Tempest*, everyone, as Gonzalo notes, leaves the island in a changed state: Alonso finally suffers the pangs of guilt and begs forgiveness for his crimes against Prospero; Antonio eventually humbles himself. These two villains are mirrored in a kind of comic relief by Trinculo and Stephano, who are also led to repentance.

Since *The Tempest* is considered Shakespeare's final great play, many critics have suggested that Prospero represents Shakespeare himself at the end of his work; that the magician's final speech, in which he renounces magic, is meant to symbolize the Bard's farewell to the theater before retiring to his Stratford home. The entire allegorical plot, beginning with an ocean-going peril and subsequently spanning the breadth of human emotions, ending in a scene of serenity and joy, may indeed reflect and symbolize the writer's reflections on his life.

At any rate, the play stands as one of Shakespeare's greatest works, possessing a strange, undefined, composite quality that sets it apart from all others.

He then took his books and staff and cast them into the sea, openly vowing to give up his long-held practice of sorcery.

As You Like It

TYPE OF WORK

Romantic comedy

SETTING

France; Duke Frederick's
court and Forest of Arden;
1500's

PRINCIPAL CHARACTERS

Duke Senior
Exiled rightful ruler

Duke Frederick
Usurper of his brother's dukedom

Oliver and Orlando
Sons of Sir Rowland de Boys

Adam
Longtime servant to Sir Rowland

Rosalind
Duke Senior's daughter

Celia
Duke Frederick's daughter

Phebe
A shepherdess

Silvius
*A shepherd with unrequited love
for Phebe*

Touchstone
*A "motley fool" jester who provides
good-humor throughout the play*

Orlando was angry with his older brother Oliver
for giving him nothing from their father's estate.
He complained loudly to Adam, an old family servant.
Just then, in walked Oliver, the object of Orlando's ire.
They quarreled, and though Adam pled with them
"for your father's remembrance" not to fight, Orlando
continued to demand his share of the inheritance –
which Oliver at last reluctantly granted in order to avoid
violence. Then, as Orlando left, Oliver drove Adam
out as well: "Get you with him, you old dog."

Left alone, Oliver summoned mighty Charles,
the court wrestler. The next day Orlando was to wrestle
Charles, and Oliver charged him, "I had as lief thou did'st
break his neck as his finger."

Meanwhile, at the court of Duke Frederick, his daughter
Celia consoled melancholy Rosalind, her cousin – and the
daughter of the recently deposed duke Senior. But Celia's
consolations were futile; Rosalind could not "forget
a banished father." Only when Celia promised that she
would turn over her whole future inheritance – the
dukedom itself – to Rosalind, did Rosalind grow "merry"
again. The cousins then decided to go watch the wrestling
match. Meeting Orlando on the way, they tried to persuade
him to "give over this attempt" at besting Charles, who
had already crushed the ribs of three challengers. But
Orlando would not be dissuaded.

The match ended quickly; to the astonishment of all, Charles was thrown and Orlando declared the victor. Duke Frederick called the champion forward to receive his reward, but upon learning that Orlando was the son of his enemy, Sir Rowland, he angrily sent the young man on his way. Rosalind, on the other hand, offered her hero a chain: "Wear this for me," she told him. Then she blushingly added, "Sir, you have wrestled well, and overthrown more than your enemies."

Just days later, Duke Frederick gruffly took Rosalind aside. "Within these ten days," he warned, "if that thou be'st found so near our public court as twenty miles, thou diest for it." Though Rosalind protested that she was not a traitor, her uncle remained unmoved. As the daughter of Duke Senior, Frederick's deposed brother, Rosalind was unwelcome in his realm. But unbeknownst to Frederick, his own daughter Celia offered to join her cousin in exile. That night the girls would depart for the Forest of Arden, where Duke Senior now lived. Since the forest was a dangerous place for two women alone, the taller Rosalind dressed as a pageboy, calling herself "Ganymede," while Celia put on the rags of a shepherdess, and called herself "Aliena." They also invited the "clownish fool of [the] court," Touchstone, to accompany them. That evening, the three fugitives escaped undetected.

Now that same night, Adam warned Orlando of Oliver's plan to burn Orlando's house, leaving him no safe refuge. Adam offered Orlando his life's savings and asked, "Let me be your servant." Orlando gladly accepted and together they, too, left for the Forest of Arden.

As Celia, Touchstone, and Rosalind – she in boy's clothing – made their way through the woods, they overheard a shepherd, Silvius, pouring out his heart to his friend Corin: "O Corin, that thou knew'st how I do love her [Phebe]!" With this, the distraught shepherd ran away. Rosalind and company, "with travel much oppressed," then approached Corin, and he extended an invitation for them to eat and rest in his own humble cottage.

Meanwhile, in another part of the woods, Adam, faint after their long journey, complained to Orlando: "Dear master … I die for food." Orlando promised he would bring victuals to the faithful old servant, or die trying. During his search, he came upon the exiled Duke Senior and his men, who were about to eat. Orlando strutted towards them and menacingly decreed, "Forebear, and eat no more!… He dies that touches any of this fruit till I and my affairs are answered." Duke Senior, unoffended, invited Orlando to sit down and join them. Then, embarrassed by his own ill-mannered behavior, Orlando begged their forgiveness and hurried to retrieve Adam. As everyone ate, Orlando revealed to Duke Senior that he was the son of Sir Rowland, whereupon the Duke exclaimed, "I am the Duke that loved your father."

Back at court, Duke Frederick, believing that Orlando had helped Celia and Rosalind escape, threatened Oliver

"Sir, you have wrestled well, and overthrown more than your enemies."

with the seizure of his lands unless he brought his brother back to him in chains. With this, he sent the young man packing for the Forest of Arden.

Now as Orlando made his way through the forest, he went about carving poems into trees declaring his love for Rosalind. Dressed as Ganymede, Rosalind found one of the verses: "Let no face be kept in mind but the fair of Rosalind." Celia also happened on one of the poems, good-naturedly teased Rosalind, and revealed that Rosalind's own Orlando was the author. Suddenly, up strode Orlando himself with one of Duke Senior's men. Rosalind – as Ganymede – decided to "play the knave with him" and addressed him "like a saucy lackey." Eventually, "Ganymede" posed a remedy for Orlando's love: Orlando was to woo Ganymede as though he were Rosalind. The "boy" would then run the gambit of emotions with

Duke Frederick … threatened Oliver with the seizure of his lands unless he brought his brother back to him in chains.

his "suitor," thereby curing him of his passion.

The next morning "Ganymede" awaited Orlando, but he failed to come. As the disguised Rosalind confided her misery to Celia, Corin came to announce the approach of Phebe and Silvius. Sure enough, Silvius appeared, once more pleading with his shepherdess – "Sweet Phebe, do not scorn me" – which only made Phebe scorn him more. Then Rosalind stepped forward to berate them both. But even as "Ganymede" chided Phebe for her disdain and scolded Silvius for putting up with it, Phebe was enchanted by "his" beauty. "I had rather hear you chide," she simpered, "than this man woo."

Finally Orlando arrived. "Orlando, where have you been all this while? You a lover?…" Rosalind wailed, as if she were a boy mimicking a lady. Orlando begged her pardon, and at last Rosalind forgave him: "Come, woo me, woo me; for now I am in a holiday humor and like enough to consent. What would you say to me now, and I were your very very Rosalind?" and they bantered back and forth until Rosalind maneuvered Orlando into asking for her hand in marriage. Orlando later departed.

Soon after, Oliver came upon the boy Ganymede, whose name he recognized. Displaying Orlando's bloody handkerchief, Oliver explained his brother's earlier delay. It seems that while Oliver napped beneath a tree, Orlando, passing by on his way to woo Ganymede, had come upon his sleeping brother – in mortal danger from a lurking lioness – and turned back to the rescue. "… Kindness, nobler even than revenge, And nature, stronger than his just occasion, made him give battle to the lioness."

> "I had rather hear you chide," she simpered, "than this man woo."

Orlando's intervention had converted his brother's hatred into love; the two were reconciled.

At the sight of Orlando's bloodstained handkerchief, however, Rosalind swooned, a most unmanly act. Though she quickly regained herself – "I pray you tell your brother how well I counterfeited" – Oliver was not fooled. "It was a passion of earnest," he was certain.

When Oliver returned to Orlando, he recounted all that had transpired. He also confessed his love for Aliena (Celia) and swore that Orlando could keep their father's entire estate; he, Oliver, would now prefer to stay in the forest to "live and die a shepherd."

Ganymede then advanced toward Orlando, offering once more to substitute for his beloved Rosalind. But Orlando could not play the part; his sadness was too deep. Filled with compassion, Ganymede promised him that on the morrow, by magical art, he would "set [Rosalind] before your eyes."

Then up walked Phebe, still in a huff, and still followed by the devoted Silvius. Ganymede once more chided her: "… You are followed by a faithful shepherd: Look upon

"Come, woo me, woo me; for now I am in a holiday humor and like enough to consent."

"You are
followed
by a faithful
shepherd:
Look upon
him, love him;
he worships
you."

him, love him; he worships you." Phebe, however, still proclaimed her love for Ganymede. So, Rosalind struck a bargain with Phebe: If on the following day Phebe still wanted to marry Ganymede, they would marry. But if Phebe refused, then she must wed the scorned Silvius. Phebe agreed.

"If sight and shape be true, why then, my love adieu!"

The next day, as all the suitors waited in the forest, Hymen, the goddess of marriage, entered the clearing with Rosalind – dressed finally as herself. Orlando was thrilled; Phebe was shocked. "If sight and shape be true, why then, my love adieu!" she wailed.

Orlando and his Rosalind, Oliver and Celia, Phebe and Silvius – and even Touchstone with Aubrey, a "homely wench" from the forest – joined hands in marriage as Hymen chirped:

Whiles a wedlock hymn we sing,
Feed yourselves with questioning,
That reason wonder may diminish
how thus we met, and these things finish.

"… Kindness, nobler even than revenge … made him give battle to the lioness."

COMMENTARY

One of Shakespeare's most famous works, *As You Like It* possesses many classic elements of comedy. The personal divisions at the outset (two Duke-brothers at war, two other brothers filled with hate for one another, daughters separated from their fathers) all strike a discordant note central to the comedic form. Moreover, the device of Rosalind being mistaken for a man creates humorous tension throughout. As in most comedies, though, by the end of the play all wrongs are somehow righted; brothers come together and every Jack has his Jill.

The Merchant of Venice

TYPE OF WORK

Comedic drama

SETTING

Renaissance Venice
and Belmont

PRINCIPAL CHARACTERS

Antonio
A Venetian merchant

Bassanio
*His young friend, in love
with Portia*

Portia
*A beautiful and wealthy
young heiress*

Shylock
A rich Jew

Jessica
Shylock's lovely daughter

Whenever Bassanio needed money he would go to his older friend Antonio, a wealthy Venetian merchant. Now Bassanio needed a sizable loan for a certain "enterprise." When questioned concerning this venture, Bassanio admitted he had fallen in love with Portia, a wealthy and famous young lady. Unless Bassanio had money, he could never hope to compete with the myriad rich noblemen and princes who vied for Portia's favor. Antonio would have gladly supplied his friend with the money, but he had no cash on hand; all of his capital was tied up in ships, not due to return from foreign ports for several weeks.

So Antonio and Bassanio found their way to Shylock, a rich Jewish moneylender who had made his fortune by charging exorbitant interest rates. Though they despised Shylock, the two managed to swallow their pride long enough to petition him to loan them three thousand ducats, to be paid back as soon as Antonio's ships returned to port. Shylock bitterly rebuked them for having the temerity to come crawling to him for a loan after publicly disdaining him:

> … *You call me a misbeliever, cut-throat dog,*
> *And spit upon my Jewish gabardine.…*
> *Well then, it now appears you need my help.…*
> *What should I say to you? Should I not say …*
> *"Fair sir, you spat on me on Wednesday last;*

You spurned me such and such day; another time
You call'd me dog; and for these courtesies
I'll lend you thus much moneys?"

Finally, though, glowing and rubbing his hands together as if he would "get to the bone" of his petitioners, Shylock agreed to lend the money, but on this condition: if the full sum were not repaid within three months, he could lawfully cut one pound of flesh from Antonio's body.

Bassanio was shocked at the proposal, but Antonio assured him there was no need to worry; his ships were expected home a full month before the debt would come due. Reluctantly, Bassanio accepted the terms of the loan.

Meanwhile, the lovely Portia had been receiving visits from prospective husbands – and she disliked them all. To make matters worse, she wasn't allowed to choose her husband for herself. Her late father had left a provision in his will that Portia's husband would be chosen by lottery. Three caskets – one of gold, one of silver, and one of lead – had been laid out, and only one of these contained a portrait of the lady. Any potential suitor must choose one of the caskets. If the casket he chose contained the portrait, he could marry Portia; if not, he would be compelled to leave and never woo another woman again. Fortunately for Portia, none of the suitors who had sought her had as yet guessed the right casket.

Elsewhere, Launcelot, Shylock's comical servant, decided he would finally escape from his master's employ; Shylock was simply too cruel to endure. Launcelot paused long enough to break the news to Jessica, Shylock's daughter, who was heartbroken to see him go. "Our house is a hell," she said, "and thou, a merry devil, Didst rob it of some taste of tediousness." Before he left, Jessica gave

Launcelot a letter to deliver to Lorenzo, a friend of Bassanio's with whom she had fallen in love. The letter instructed Lorenzo to meet her at her house, where she would escape in disguise and elope with him. That night, Jessica and Lorenzo carried out their lovers' plan, fleeing the city in a gondola filled with Shylock's ducats. When Shylock learned that his daughter had run away to marry a Christian, he was at once crushed and furious, and grew all the more fervent in his hatred of Antonio and his Christian friends.

In the meantime, Bassanio had made his way to Portia, ready to hazard a try at the caskets. Portia immediately fell in love with him and feared lest he should choose the wrong box. But, guided by Portia's sea-blue eyes, Bassanio avoided the temptation to choose the gold or silver caskets,

Though they despised Shylock, the two managed to swallow their pride long enough to petition him to loan them three thousand ducats …

and, wisely declaring, "All that glitters is not gold," correctly selected the unassuming lead. Both Portia and Bassanio were elated. But no sooner were their wedding plans underway than they were interrupted by horrifying news from Venice: every one of Antonio's ships had been shipwrecked in a storm, leaving him penniless and unable to pay his debt to Shylock. Shylock would now obtain the revenge he sought. In a pathetic letter to Bassanio, Antonio resigned himself to his fate and bade farewell to his friend.

Bassanio and Portia postponed their marriage and rushed to Venice to aid their benefactor. But what could they do? Antonio had agreed to the contract of his own free will; and Shylock would surely insist on carrying out the penalty. The law was on his side.

It was Portia, after deep thought, who hatched a plot to save her husband's friend. Knowing that he would have to appear in court to either pay his debt or announce his default, Portia decided to masquerade herself as a young lawyer sent to act in Antonio's defense.

Antonio's ships had been shipwrecked in a storm, leaving him penniless and unable to pay his debt to Shylock.

The day of the trial finally arrived. Antonio confessed to the Duke, acting as judge, that he could not pay his debt, and that he was prepared to allow the moneylender to exact his pound of flesh. The Duke and all those present at the court begged Shylock to spare Antonio, but he refused. Bassanio – now a rich man because of his betrothal to Portia – offered Shylock "thrice the sum" of Antonio's debt, but still Shylock preferred that Antonio should die, insisting, "I would have my bond." The Duke, bound by law, sadly admitted that the penalty was valid.

> The quality of mercy is not strained, it droppeth as the gentle rain from heaven ...

At that moment, Portia, pretending to be "Balthasar," a lawyer sent by the respected but ill Doctor Bellario, entered the court to defend Antonio. In an elegant speech, she encouraged Shylock to lay aside the letter of the law in favor of mercy:

> *The quality of mercy is not strained –*
> *It droppeth as the gentle rain from heaven*
> *Upon the place beneath: it is twice blessed, –*
> *It blesseth him that gives, and him that takes....*

But Shylock would have none of it. "I crave the law!" he raved. Next, Portia asked if anyone would pay Antonio's bond, and this time Bassanio offered to pay ten times the debt. But once more Shylock refused, and insisted that justice be carried out.

Portia now changed her stance. She craftily pretended to agree with the Jew. If he insisted on the letter of the law, it must be carried out: "A pound of that ... merchant's flesh is thine; the court awards it, and the law doth give it."

… the contract stated that Shylock was to extract "a pound of flesh" – but mentioned nothing about blood.

Then she ordered a knife be brought. Shylock was ecstatic to find this defender in agreement with him, and raised his knife to inflict the fatal wound to his enemy's breast. But just then, Portia interjected to remind Shylock of one detail: the words in the contract stated that Shylock was to extract "a pound of flesh" – but mentioned nothing about blood. Therefore, if in cutting into Antonio's heart Shylock should shed even one drop of blood, he would violate the contract, and, by the laws of Venice, he must be executed and his lands confiscated.

Astonished and trembling, Shylock dropped the knife and scowled. The court rang with laughter.

Shylock offered to let Antonio go in peace, but Portia refused. After all, since he insisted on the letter of the law, he must have it. Now it was Shylock who pled for mercy. The court decided to spare his life, but to confiscate his lands (reserving half for his daughter after his death) and to force him to adopt Christianity. Shylock slumped from the courtroom, humiliated and bitter.

Jubilant, Antonio and his friends were soon made aware of Portia's cunning disguise. All returned to Belmont, where Bassanio and fair Portia established their new household.

COMMENTARY

As with many of Shakespeare's plays, the titular protagonist of *The Merchant of Venice* (Antonio) plays a relatively minor role in the action. Bassanio and Portia are more central characters, but even they are upstaged by the brilliant and perplexing character of Shylock.

How is the audience or reader meant to react to Shylock? He ought to strike us as thoroughly loathsome – he is a usurer, an abusive parent, violent, legalistic, bitter, unsociable and greedy. In spite of all these faults, though, one cannot help feeling some sympathy for him. After all, he is forced to live among neighbors who neither understand nor respect his religious beliefs; avowed "Christians" who treat him with cruelty. Forced into his money-lending by legal restrictions on Jewish professions, he remains highly intelligent and capable of great eloquence, as in this passionate complaint against Antonio's abuses:

> He hath ... laught at my losses, mockt at my gains, scorn'd my nation, thwarted my bargains, cooled my friends, heated mine enemies; and what's his reason? I am a Jew. Hath not a Jew eyes? hath not a Jew hands, organs, dimensions, senses, affections, passions? fed with the same food, hurt with the same weapons, subject to the same diseases, healed by the same means, warmed and cooled by the same winter and summer, as a Christian is? If you

Hath not a Jew eyes? hath not a Jew hands, organs, dimensions, sense, affections, passions?

prick us, do we not bleed? if you tickle us, do we not laugh? if you poison us, do we not die? And if you wrong us, shall we not revenge?…

Marvelous lines, and in some respects a more compassionate speech than uttered by any of the Christian characters. So, Shylock is an ambiguous villain.

But the play is not Shylock's story; it is a comedy, and the triumph of mercy over unyielding justice is the theme that finally brings *The Merchant of Venice* to its happy resolution.

Much Ado About Nothing

TYPE OF WORK

Romantic comedy

SETTING

Messina, Italy;
Sixteenth century

PRINCIPAL CHARACTERS

Don Pedro
Prince of Arragon

Don John
His jealous brother

Claudio
*A young Florentine lord loyal
to Don Pedro*

Benedick
*A witty bachelor and another ally
of Pedro*

Leonato
Governor of Messina

Hero
Leonato's daughter

Beatrice
*Hero's cousin, also known for her
sharp wit*

Borachio
Aide to Don John

After quashing the attempt of his bastard brother John
to take control of Arragon, Don Pedro, bound for home
with his two friends Claudio and Benedick, neared
Messina. There, Governor Leonato, his daughter, Hero,
and her cousin Beatrice, waited at the city gate to welcome
both the victors and the defeated. Don John, as part of the
truce, had agreed that Pedro would indeed rule Arragon;
Pedro in turn agreed to permit John to return to his
holdings there in peace. Leonato beamed to see Pedro on
his way home with few casualties – and reconciled with
his brother as well. Beatrice, on the other hand, felt mixed
emotions on greeting Benedick, Pedro's ally and her
own wordy rival. "There is a merry war betwixt Signior
Benedick and her …" Leonato noted. "A skirmish of wits
between them."

After formally greeting the victorious Pedro,
the governor invited him and his entourage to stay in
Messina with his family for a few days before pushing on
to Arragon. On the way to Leonato's house, however,
Benedick and Claudio lagged far behind; Claudio wished
to solicit Benedick's opinion of Hero. To Claudio she
was the sweetest lady he had ever laid eyes on. When Pedro,
returning to hurry the two along, was told of Claudio's
infatuation with Hero, he consented to help him
gain favor with her; he would act as intermediary on
Claudio's behalf.

Now, a passerby loyal to Don John happened to overhear this conversation, and promptly informed his master of Claudio's desires to marry Hero. "That young upstart hath all the glory of my overthrow," John sneered. "If I can cross him any way, I bless myself every way." And so, Don John launched his plot against Claudio – and his attack against his powerful brother.

> "That young upstart hath all the glory of my overthrow … If I can cross him any way, I bless myself every way."

That night at a masked celebration, it was agreed that Pedro would woo Hero for Claudio. All went as planned – until Don John made insinuating remarks, well within Claudio's range of hearing, hinting that Pedro, even as he ostensibly courted Hero on Claudio's behalf, actually intended to keep her for himself. Claudio became distraught. By the time Pedro arrived to break the good news – Hero and Claudio were to be married – Claudio had fled, irate and humiliated, acting like "a schoolboy who, being overjoyed with finding a bird's nest, shows it his companion and he steals it." But at length Beatrice found the pouting Claudio, reasoned with him, and brought him back.

Later, in a gleeful, mischievous scheme, Hero, Claudio, Pedro and Leonato decided to do some further matchmaking. They resolved that Benedick, a confirmed and contented bachelor, and Beatrice, a girl equally opposed to matrimony, would be impossible to match as husband and wife. So they undertook the devious challenge of bringing these two argumentative souls together before resuming their journey to Arragon.

That very afternoon, while Benedick strolled in the palace's garden, Claudio, Pedro and Leonato, pretending not to see him, sat lamenting poor Beatrice, so tortured by her love for Benedick. At the same time, Hero and her handmaiden walked through an orchard, and, knowing that Beatrice was hidden there, solemnly talked of how inwardly tormented Benedick was by his unrequited love for Beatrice. The plan worked perfectly. The next time the two "merry rivals" united, instead of trading the usual insults and quarrels, each determined to console the other's supposed passion.

Meanwhile, John, having learned of the forthcoming marriage of Claudio and Hero, conspired anew. He sent his aide, Borachio, to fool Claudio into believing that Hero had another lover.

That evening, John lured Claudio and Pedro to a place near the window of Hero's bedchamber. Borachio had persuaded one of Hero's servants to dress in her mistress's clothing. In pretense of wooing Hero, Borachio then went through the motions of seducing the maid, casting their embracing shadow on the window. Upon witnessing this,

… in a gleeful, mischievous plan … they undertook the devious challenge of bringing these two argumentative souls together …

Claudio and Pedro grew livid, but decided to wait until the wedding to properly denounce the faithless Hero.

A nightwatchman later overheard Borachio bragging about his duplicity and arrested him. But in their stupidity, the town officials failed to reveal the plot in time to stay Hero's fall from grace. On the next morning, as the wedding vows were being taken, Claudio suddenly refused his bride. "There, Leonato," he told the governor, "take her back again. Give not this rotten orange to your friend.… She knows the heat of a luxurious bed." The wedding guests were stunned. Of course Hero denied everything, but to no avail. And then, flushed with disgrace, she swooned and fainted. Even Leonato accepted Claudio's eyewitness account of her betrayal. She has "fallen into a pit of ink, that the wide sea hath drops too few to wash her clean again," the father mourned. Nevertheless, before Leonato could disown his daughter, the friar performing the ceremony intervened. He believed in Hero's integrity, and counseled Leonato to have patience and trust. Then in a plan of his own, he convinced Leonato to give Hero a chance to "change slander to remorse." The father was to

"Give not this rotten orange to your friend.… She knows the heat of a luxurious bed."

Though their talk was still filled with wit and jibes, now it was tempered with genuine affection.

hide his daughter's slumped body away and let out word that she was dead. Meanwhile, the friar would seek evidence to prove her innocence. The two men then carried Hero out of the room, leaving only Benedick and Beatrice in the marriage hall. Though their talk was still filled with wit and jibes, now it was tempered with genuine affection. Benedick remarked: "I do love nothing in the world so well as you. Is not that strange?" But Beatrice held back her proclamations of love. She would not commit to him. First, to test his love, she made him promise to kill Claudio, the villain who had "slandered, scorned, dishonored [her] kinswoman."

In the meantime, the constable had arrested Borachio and brought him before the town sexton for questioning. After listening to the story, the sexton elected to take Borachio before Leonato so that he too could hear how Hero had been wronged. Unfortunately, Leonato and his older brother were already taking matters into their own hands. According to plan, they sought out Claudio and Pedro and challenged them to fight: "Thou hast killed my child. If thou kill'st me, boy, thou shall kill a man." But neither Pedro nor Claudio wanted any part of sending two elderly gentlemen to their deaths; they refused the challenge and went on their way.

Next, Benedick met Claudio and Pedro. He too dared the slanderous Claudio to duel. And still, Claudio refused the challenge.

Just then up marched the constable, leading Borachio toward Leonato's palace. Claudio and Pedro were told of what had actually happened the night before; they had been tricked – and Hero defamed – by the plot of wicked Don John. That very night these two sought to take revenge, but John had fled the city.

Also that night, Leonato, now informed about the truth behind his daughter's broken marriage ceremony, demanded that Claudio stand before him. He told Claudio that he could be forgiven of his offense against his dead daughter on two conditions: first, he must publicly confess Hero's innocence to all Messina and "hang an epitaph upon her tomb, and sing it to her bones"; secondly, he must marry Leonato's niece, who was "almost the copy" of Hero. Claudio gladly embraced Leonato's two requisites for penance.

The following morning, after Claudio had sung to an empty tomb, he and his unknown bride-to-be stood side by side in the marriage hall. Then, as the veil was lifted away from her face, Claudio discovered to his overwhelming joy his own beloved Hero – alive! The friar calmed the ecstatic groom and promised to explain the whole affair once the ceremony was finished.

… as the veil was lifted away from her face, Claudio discovered to his overwhelming joy his own beloved Hero – alive!

Attending the wedding were Benedick and Beatrice – naturally, matching wits again. In the course of their bantering, Benedick asked Beatrice why she did not show her love for him; after all, Leonato, Claudio and Pedro had indeed spoken of her feelings. In like manner, Beatrice insisted that Hero and her handmaiden must have been sorely deceived, for they had also sworn that Benedick loved her. Eventually, the pair of rivals did admit (reluctantly) that perhaps it was true – maybe they did love one another.

Before the procession could depart the chapel, Benedick called everyone together and announced that he and Beatrice were ready to wed.

That day, the double wedding, coupled with word that Don John had been captured, made Pedro's heart a merry one. And before leaving the chapel, the overjoyed Benedick gave Pedro, suddenly the sole bachelor among the three friends, some advice: "Get thee a wife, get thee a wife!"

Eventually, the pair of rivals did admit (reluctantly) that perhaps it was true – maybe they did love one another.

COMMENTARY

Throughout *Much Ado About Nothing*, Shakespeare artfully combines comedy with near-tragedy. To complete his tapestry of interwoven plots, the resolution had to be brilliantly contrived. Some students of Shakespeare believe that, as one of the Bard's final comedies, this work inspired within him renewed moral consciousness. And indeed his tragic dramas from this point on focus on themes of ethical transgression and human weakness that had served only as fragmented bits of plots in previous plays.

Much Ado is fraught with allusions to the symbol of cuckoldry – the horns a husband (Claudio) must wear when his wife has had an adulterous affair. For Benedick as well, the fear of wearing "horns" on his head spawns many of his witticisms concerning marriage.

Often in Shakespeare's comedies, a strong woman such as Beatrice will at some point don men's clothing, as a sign of strength and equality in a man's world. However, Beatrice uses only her wit to protect her – a more than ample weapon. Men flee her cruel tongue as though it were a "drawn sword" or a "ferocious lion." The plot includes suggestions of violence, treachery and sorrow throughout; but, in the end, the schemes and threats amount merely to "much ado about nothing."

All's Well That Ends Well

TYPE OF WORK

Dramatic comedy

SETTING

Medieval France and Italy

PRINCIPAL CHARACTERS

Bertram
A young aristocrat

The Countess of Rousillon
Bertram's mother

Helena
*Attendant to the Countess
of Rousillon*

Lafeu
A French lord

The King of France

Diana
*A beautiful young Florentine who
befriends Helena*

Soon after the death of the Count of Rousillon, the Count's great friend – who also happened to be King of France – came down with a disease which the court physicians were unable to cure. Fearing that his own death was imminent, the childless King sent for his late friend's only child, Bertram, who was now his ward. The Countess of Rousillon was much aggrieved by her son's summons. "In delivering my son from me," she wailed, "I bury a second husband." But the French lord Lafeu, who had come to take Bertram, reassured her that the King would conduct himself like a father toward her son.

A wise and kind-hearted woman, the Countess finally reconciled herself to her son's departure. Realizing the import of his bearing before the court, she composed herself to leave him with some motherly advice:

> *Be thou blessed, Bertram, and succeed thy father*
> *In manners as in shape! Thy blood and virtue*
> *Contend for empire in thee, and thy goodness*
> *Share with thy birthright! Love all, trust a few,*
> *Do wrong to none....*

Though her son was very dear to her, the Countess also mourned aloud at how young he was – and how filled with vanity and self-importance. And as if to obligingly illustrate these unattractive aspects of his character, after bidding farewell to his mother, Bertram turned to her servant, Helena, the orphaned daughter of a physician, and reminded the girl contemptuously that in his absence she had better pamper her mistress.

Unbeknownst to Bertram, however, Helena was in love with him and was very greatly saddened at his leaving. But Helena was a resourceful maid and she quickly devised a plan to follow Bertram to the king's court to win him for her husband. She would cure the king with a secret prescription that her late father, a highly respected physician, had willed to her at his death.

"Why Helen, thou shalt have my leave and love," the Countess told the girl when she learned of the plan. And indeed the Countess did love Helena very much. "I am a mother to you," the warmhearted woman rehearsed to her young attendant. Convinced of her patroness's trust and affection, Helena set off for court.

At first the King was reluctant to try Helena's remedy. But Helena persisted; if the cure failed, she proclaimed, "with vilest torture let my life be ended." Hearing these words, the monarch reconsidered. Would this "kind maid" truly offer her life to him if the prescription were inferior? Finally he told her, "I will try."

Clever girl that she was, Helena then asked the King what he proposed to give her in return, should the cure prove effective. Whatever she desired, he replied. Helena responded that she wished to choose a husband from among the eligible bachelors at court. "My deed shall match thy deed," he promised.

Helena's prescription did indeed cure the King. He was exuberant. Leading Helena in a spirited dance into the

Helena was a resourceful maid and she quickly devised a plan to follow Bertram to the king's court to win him for her husband.

palace's Great Hall, he ordered Lafeu to "Go, call before
me all the lords in court." Then, with the court assembled,
he turned to Helena:

> *Fair maid, send forth thine eye: this youthful parcel*
> *Of noble bachelors stand at my bestowing,*
> *O'er whom both sovereign power and father's voice*
> *I have to use: thy frank election make;*
> *Thou has power to choose, and they have none to forsake.*

Helena did not single out Bertram immediately. She first
approached various courtiers, both to test their obedience
to their ruler's command and to build her confidence.
"Sir, will you hear my suit?" she asked them one by one.
Each assured her that he would. When at last, however,
she dared to confess that her choice was Bertram, the
young count protested. Incredulous at Bertram's reaction,
the King addressed him: "Know'st thou not, Bertram, what
she has done for me?" Yes, Bertram knew – but even after

Fair maid, send
forth thine eye.
This young parcel …
Of noble bachelors
stand at my
bestowing …

He would never think of Helena as his wife ... unless she could fulfill two seemingly impossible conditions ...

the King had pointed out how "young, wise and fair"
Helena was, the pompous aristocrat could not wipe away
his "disdain" for her humble upbringing. Angry with
Bertram's arrogance and impudence, the King chastened
the lad:

> … *That is honor's scorn,*
> *Which challenges itself as honor's born*
> *And is not like the sire: honors thrive,*
> *When rather from our acts we them derive.…*

But Bertram still refused, objecting that he did not love the
lowly girl. To make the match sweeter to the headstrong
young man, the frustrated King bestowed a rich dowry
on Helena, equal to or greater than Bertram's own estate.
Finally, seeing that he had no real choice in the matter,
Bertram agreed, and he and Helena were wed.

But Bertram had resolved that he would never live with
Helena; instead, he would go to war to fight on behalf of
the Duke of Florence. That same day, with the help of his
trusted, though unscrupulous, friend Parolles, Bertram
composed a letter to his new bride, explaining that he
was off to war and demanding her immediate removal
from court. He would never think of Helena as his wife,
Bertram informed her, unless she could fulfill two
seemingly impossible conditions: *When thou canst get the
ring upon my finger which never shall come off, and show me
a child begotten of thy body that I am father to, then call me
husband: but in such a 'then' I write a 'never.'*

Returning home to Rousillon as Bertram had charged,
Helena found the Countess waiting to comfort her.
The kind woman deplored her son's treatment of his new
wife. But now Helena, still devoted to Bertram and certain

that he would not return home to his mother from the battle if she remained there, decided to escape Rousillon for a time. Leaving the Countess a letter stating that she had gone on a religious pilgrimage, Helena set off for Italy.

On her way, Helena stopped in Florence, staying at the house of a widow and her lovely young daughter, Diana. All three of them, it appeared by their conversation, were acquainted with Bertram.

At first Helena did not reveal her true identity; she simply listened as the other women chatted. It turned out that Bertram had earlier pursued Diana, but that she had spurned him – and, so she had heard, recently married. Now, Diana could feel nothing but compassion for the poor lady who had married him, and contempt for his companion, the "vile rascal" Parolles.

Convinced that she was in sympathetic company, Helena finally revealed herself as Bertram's new bride. Would the mother and daughter give her "good aid"? she asked. Would they help her fulfill the terms of Bertram's letter? Indeed they would – particularly after Helena had presented them with a "purse of gold."

Diana found Bertram, advised him that she had reconsidered his proposition, and agreed to meet him in her chamber at midnight. But in exchange for her "chastity," she told him, he would have to agree to her terms: to trade his ring for hers and to refrain from speech in her bedroom. Bertram, overjoyed at the thought of lying with his lady-love, agreed. Unbeknownst to Bertram, however, as midnight approached, Helena took Diana's place in the dark room, and waited to exchange her ring for his.

Bertram was easily deceived; innocently, he spent the night with Helena. But still another deception awaited the susceptible Bertram: Helena had arranged to have news of her death reach her husband. And thus, believing her safely out of his way forever, Bertram at last returned home.

The King, the Countess and Lafeu were all assembled at Rousillon when he arrived. All mourned Helena; seeing their sorrow, even Bertram himself had a change of heart and professed his love for his departed wife. Moved by Bertram's declaration, the King forgave him of his harsh treatment of her:

> *Our rash faults*
> *Make trivial price of serious things we have,*
> *Not knowing them until we know their grave:*
> *Oft our displeasures, to ourselves unjust,*
> *Destroy our friends and after weep their dust....*

But no sooner had the King finished speaking than he noticed the ring on Bertram's finger – the very ring the King had once given to Helena as a gift. Translating this to

Convinced that she was in sympathetic company, Helena finally revealed herself as Bertram's new bride.

mean that Helena's life had been "foully snatched," the monarch became infuriated.

Just then, in order to save Bertram's life, Diana burst into the room and recited the story of how she had arranged a darkened tryst with him where she had received his ring. "To prison with her!" ordered the King, bewildered and outraged.

... seeing their sorrow, even Bertram himself had a change of heart and professed his love for his departed wife.

And then, a moment later, Helena herself appeared. "Is't real that I see?" the King wondered aloud. For his part, Bertram immediately begged Helena's forgiveness. Helena, reminding Bertram of the terms of his letter, then pointed to the ring and revealed that she was expecting his child. "Will you be mine," she asked, "now you are doubly won?" And Bertram vowed that he truly would "love her dearly."

The King again pledged to pay Helena's dowry and, recalling all the troubles of the past, concluded that joy was very welcome indeed.

COMMENTARY

Throughout its history, *All's Well That Ends Well* has presented critics with problems of classification. In the strictest sense, the work is neither drama nor comedy; it seems to impart the kind of moral lesson that drama often presents, but also includes many farcical moments. Displaying little gaiety or romance, preferring instead to convey through comedy Shakespeare's decidedly troubled view of mankind's imperfections, "Dark Comedy," then, is the term most frequently used to categorize the play.

But what is the moral lesson portrayed, the reader may ask? First and foremost, *All's Well* emphasizes that virtue – not title, position or lineage – reaps the ultimate reward. Clearly, the plucky and persevering Helena's virtue – which the Countess praises early in the play and which the King recognizes as "wisdom" and "courage" – has won Bertram's affection by play's end. Not only has she demonstrated her steadfast loyalty to Bertram (a somewhat unattractive prize), but she has succeeded in outwitting him. Providing both the most dramatic and the most comic elements of the play, this devotion often takes a remarkably selfless form. Before leaving on her pilgrimage, for instance, she repents of her willfulness and sympathizes with Bertram:

> *… Poor Lord! Is't I*
> *That chase thee from thy country and expose*
> *Those tender limbs of thine to the event*
> *Of the none-sparing war?*

Herein, Helena demonstrates her maturity. She – like the older characters, the King and the Countess – finds her dignity in caring for others, a virtue that has nothing to do with the circumstances of her birth. Life is not, after all, how all begins, but rather how "all ends" that matters.

A Midsummer Night's Dream

TYPE OF WORK

Comedic drama

SETTING

Athens, in ancient Greece

PRINCIPAL CHARACTERS

Theseus
Duke of Athens

Hermia and Lysander
Lovers

Demetrius
Another of Hermia's wooers

Helena
Hermia's friend, who is in love with Demetrius

Oberon and Titania
The Fairy King and Queen

Puck
Oberon's servant

Theseus, Duke of Athens, impatiently anticipated his
marriage to Hippolyta, Queen of the Amazons.
His drifting thoughts were interrupted by the arrival of
Egeus, an Athenian citizen, accompanied by his beautiful
daughter Hermia and two young men. "Full of vexation
come I," Egeus complained. He wanted his daughter
to marry Demetrius, one of the young men who escorted
him, but Hermia loved the other, Lysander. Complicating
matters, both Lysander and Demetrius adored Hermia.

Theseus entreated Hermia to not be troublesome,
and ordered her to comply with her father's wishes or else
suffer, by Athenian law, one of two consequences: death,
or life without a husband. Hermia, however, took matters
into her own hands. She and Lysander, meeting in secret
soon after, decided to flee to his aunt's house – which lay
outside the jurisdiction of Athenian law. Elated with their
plan, they revealed it to Hermia's good friend Helena:

> *And in the wood, where often you and I*
> *Upon faint primrose beds were wont to lie,*
> *Emptying our bosoms of their counsel sweet,*
> *There my Lysander and myself shall meet....*

Helena listened thoughtfully. Hermia was truly her dearest
friend, but she held Demetrius – Lysander's rival – in
dearer esteem than any mere friendship. But no matter

how hard she had tried, Helena had been unable to win his affections; Demetrius remained utterly smitten with Hermia.

Weighing Hermia's confidences, Helena decided that since she could not capture Demetrius for herself, she could at least please him by helping him win his chosen love. "I will go tell him of fair Hermia's flight," she resolved.

It was a glorious Midsummer's Eve when Hermia and Lysander met for their covert forest rendezvous. On that magical evening, however, the woods swarmed with many other presences. Demetrius had come in search of Hermia – and Helena had secretly followed Demetrius. A troupe of Athenian actors also was gathered among the trees to rehearse Pyramus and Thisby, a tragedy they hoped to perform at Theseus's wedding. And, finally, there was a

Theseus ... ordered her to comply with her father's wishes or else suffer, by Athenian law, one of two consequences: either death or life without a husband.

throng of fairies meeting in the woods to join in the revels of Oberon, the Fairy King.

Oberon felt peevish that night. He and his Queen, Titania, were quarreling.

Oberon felt peevish that night. He and his Queen, Titania, were quarreling. Oberon wanted for his own Titania's pet courier and protégé, the Indian boy whom she always kept close by her side. Titania refused: the whole of Fairy Land would not be payment enough.

Now, Oberon intended to use his power as Fairy King to force Titania to comply. He directed his servant, Puck – who adored impish pranks – to find a "western flower" so that he could place the "juice of it on [the] sleeping eyelids" of his Queen. When she opened her eyes, Oberon merrily explained, she would fall in love with the first thing she gazed on – "be it on lion, bear, or wolf, or bull."

No sooner had Puck disappeared to find the wondrous flower, than Oberon spied Demetrius and Helena in a meadow. Clearly visible in the moonlight, Helena was chasing the callous young man. "I am sick when I do look on thee," Demetrius railed at poor Helena. The lovesick maid continued her pursuit: "I'll follow thee, and make a heaven of hell," she called after the fleeing youth. Oberon's heart went out to Helena. When Puck returned with the magical flower, the King instructed him to steal quietly near Demetrius while he slept and anoint his eyes with juice of the flower. When awakened, Demetrius would look upon Helena and love her.

Having sent Puck off on his mischievous errand, Oberon waited while Titania's attendants lulled their mistress to sleep; then he crept near with his magical potion and shook it gently onto the queen's dreamy eyelids. "Wake when some vile thing is near," Oberon gleefully charged his wife.

Puck, meanwhile, searching the woods for his quarry, came across a young man in Athenian garments – Oberon's description of Demetrius – stretched out asleep on the ground beside a young woman. Puck sprinkled his potion on the Athenian's eyelids and sped away to meet Oberon. Puck, however, had blundered – the lying couple on the ground were Hermia and Lysander, not Helena and Demetrius.

When Lysander awoke, Helena, disheveled and breathless from chasing Demetrius, wandered into view. The magical juice worked all too well: Lysander fell instantly in love with Helena and denounced the "tedious minutes" he had passed with Hermia. Helena, dazed by Lysander's endearments, warily assumed that Lysander was mocking her. "O, that a lady of one man refused,"

When she opened her eyes … she would fall in love with the first thing she gazed on – "be it on lion, bear, or wolf, or bull."

It was a glorious Midsummer's Eve when Hermia and Lysander met for their secret forest rendezvous.

she chastised him, "should of another therefore be abused!" Then she stormed off – with Lysander, still under the spell, hurrying after her.

Hermia awoke moments later, distraught from a nightmare: "Methought a serpent [did] eat my heart away." Noticing Lysander's disappearance, she feared for his life and hurried off to look for him.

Not far away, meanwhile, the actors were about to begin the rehearsal of their play. "Speak, Pyramus, Thisby stand forth," intoned the director. But, while Bottom, the thespian playing the role of Pyramus, waited in a thicket for his entry, the ever-mischievous Puck slyly slipped an ass's head over his mask. When on cue Bottom stepped from the thicket, the huge mask so startled the other actors that they ran away in panic. Bottom, unaware of his appearance, speculated that the company, as a joke, was trying to frighten him by leaving him alone in the woods. Thus, resolving to show no fear whatsoever, he ambled along the pathway, singing bravely.

Presently, back in Fairy Land, Titania opened her groggy eyes. "What angel wakes me from my flow'ry bed?" she asked. But it was no angel who stood before her: her gaze had alighted on none other than the actor, Bottom – looking very much like an ass. Overcome by this angelic beast, she instantly proclaimed her ardent love. Bottom, confused but pleased by this enchanting beauty's passionate confession, mused how "reason and love keep little company." Enraptured, Titania led the man with an ass's head away to her bower.

When Puck – who knew everything that went on in the woods – related to Oberon that Titania had become infatuated with a "monster," the Fairy King was elated. However, the arrival of Demetrius and Hermia, who were arguing about Lysander, interrupted his good mood. Hermia accused Demetrius of having murdered her lover in a jealous rage, and refused to believe Demetrius's denials. Hermia hastened off in alarm; Demetrius, perturbed, lay down and fell asleep. To set matters straight, Oberon sprinkled fairy juice on Demetrius's sleeping eyes, and sent Puck to make sure that Helena would be by his side when he awakened.

The plan worked. Seeing Helena, Demetrius raved, "O Helen, goddess, nymph, perfect, divine!" But at that moment, Lysander also reappeared to claim Helena as his own. Now Helena was even more bewildered than before: both men – these who had previously pursued only Hermia – fiercely proclaimed their devotion.

The magical juice worked all too well: Lysander fell instantly in love with Helena and denounced the "tedious minutes" he had passed with Hermia.

To confuse matters even further, Hermia suddenly stumbled onto the scene, looking on in puzzlement. How could her beloved Lysander suddenly claim to "hate" her and adore Helena? At last, she turned her rage on Helena, her apparent supplanter. "You juggler! You canker blossom!" Hermia lashed out, even as Lysander and Demetrius continued hurling insults at one another.

Seeing what "knaveries" his servant had caused, Oberon once again sent Puck off to set matters straight. Puck managed, after some difficulty, to herd the four exhausted Athenians into a clearing. After Lysander fell asleep on the grass, he once again applied the juice to the eyes of the slumbering lover. "The man shall have his mare again," he whispered as he dashed away, "and all shall be well."

Puck found Oberon sleeping at Titania's side. Her devotion to Bottom – that peculiar man with an ass's head – had rekindled Oberon's tenderness toward his Queen. When Titania awoke, the love spell was broken, and she

Now Helena was even more bewildered than before: both men fiercely proclaimed their devotion.

promised to give her husband the Indian boy he had wanted for a courier. Oberon said:

Seeing Helena, Demetrius raved, "O Helen, goddess, nymph, perfect, divine!"

Now thou and I are new in amity,
And will tomorrow midnight solemnly
Dance in Duke Theseus' house triumphantly,
And bless it to all fair prosperity.

Dawn lighted the sky. All had at last been set right. Lysander once more adored Hermia, and the "object and the pleasure" of Demetrius's eyes was Helena. The marriage became a triple wedding, and the actors assembled to perform their play. Just before they were to go on stage, Bottom appeared. He did not tell them about the wondrous "dream" he had witnessed or how he had spent the night in the woods. How could he? "Man is but an ass," he mused, "if he go about to expound this dream." Perhaps, someday, he would commission the troupe's director to write a ballet about it: "It shall be called," he said to himself, "'Bottom's Dream,' because it hath no bottom."

The play began. The actors stumbled and botched the performance so completely that the tragedy became comedy – leaving the three married couples greatly amused. "This palpable-gross play hath well beguiled," Theseus told the actors. Then he turned to the other couples – and to his new wife – and said, "Sweet friends, to bed."

Everyone left the festivities, delighted. Oberon and Puck appeared – in fairy garb, of course – to celebrate the nuptial feast. Pleased to see such a joyous outcome,

Oberon proclaimed that the "bride bed" of each couple would "blessed be" with happiness and children.

COMMENTARY

A *Midsummer Night's Dream* has been called Shakespeare's happiest work – and perhaps one of the happiest, most enchanting works ever written. The congenial confusion that results from the plot's comic

The play began. The actors stumbled and botched the performance so completely that the tragedy became comedy – leaving the three married couples greatly amused.

convolutions serves not to obstruct romance, but to heighten anticipation of its impending pleasures.

For instance, Egeus's forbidding his daughter Hermia to marry Lysander – even going so far as to attach a penalty of death to his objections – is so utterly arbitrary that it seems impossible to imagine how his objections cannot be overcome. The way in which Hermia and Helena triumph over the obstacles to their marriage desires serves to resolve the dramatic tension in a comic way.

The play evokes in us a nostalgia for a lost, but pagan, paradise. Unlike the familiar and darker pathos of the Biblical Eden, the paradise of *A Midsummer Night's Dream* is one in which the circumstances of love's dawning are entirely happy, and its consequences are – as Oberon says at play's end – entirely "blessed."

The Comedy of Errors

TYPE OF WORK

Farcical comedy

SETTING

Ephesus, an ancient port city in Asia Minor

PRINCIPAL CHARACTERS

Aegeon
A merchant of Syracuse

Aemilia
Aegeon's wife and abbess at Ephesus

Antipholus of Syracuse and Antipholus of Ephesus
Twin sons of Aegeon and Aemilia

Dromio of Syracuse and Dromio of Ephesus
Twin brothers and bondsmen to the two Antipholuses

Adriana
Wife to Antipholus of Ephesus

Luciana
Adriana's sister

Solinus
Duke of Ephesus

Aegeon arrived in Ephesus, after five years at sea, to find himself sentenced to death. As a result of recent animosity between Ephesus and Aegeon's native Syracuse, citizens of one city would be put to death if discovered in the other, unless a 1000-mark ransom was paid to buy his liberty. Since Aegeon could not afford the ransom, he was to be hanged at sunset.

Aegeon, sadly, did not dispute his sentence. Indeed, he welcomed it as a means "by the doom of death [to] end woes and all." When Solinus, the Duke of Ephesus, asked the merchant his motive for coming there, Aegeon replied:

> *A heavier task could not have been impos'd*
> *Than I to speak my griefs unspeakable;*
> *Yet, that the world may witness that my end*
> *Was wrought by nature, not by vile offence,*
> *I'll utter what my sorrow gives me leave.*

Aegeon then recounted the dismal, strange story behind his arrival in Ephesus. Long ago in Syracuse, the merchant had wed his beloved Aemilia. Six months later, he was forced to travel on business. Aemilia soon joined him, and while they were abroad, she bore fine twin sons, "the one so like the other as could not be distinguish'd." At "that very hour, and in the self-same inn," another woman also gave birth to identical twin sons. The parents of these twins, however, were exceedingly poor, so Aegeon bought their sons from them, intending to raise them as servants for his more favored sons.

As the young family sailed home to Syracuse, a storm arose. The mother secured one of her infant sons and one of the infant servants to one end of the mast while Aegeon did likewise with the other son and servant at the other end. When the ship sank, the floating mast struck a rock, separating the family. Because of his wife's lesser weight, Aegeon explained, the part of the mast to which she clung "was carried with more speed before the wind." Aemilia's helpless assembly of soggy boys was picked up by one ship, Aegeon's by another. Tragically, the ship that rescued Aegeon and his charges could not catch up to the vessel that had rescued Aemilia. The family seemed irrevocably severed, neither trio knowing the other's fate.

Aegeon returned to Syracuse with the two boys he had been spared, and raised them as best he could. Antipholus, however, "at eighteen years became inquisitive after his lost brother; and importun'd me that his attendant [named

Antipholus ...
at eighteen years
became inquisitive
after his lost
brother ...

Dromio] … might bear him company in the quest of him." Aegeon hesitantly complied; he desired to regain his lost son, but greatly feared losing the one that had been left to him. In the end, however, Antipholus and Dromio had set out to find their lost brothers. But as the months of their absence lengthened, Aegeon's anxiety grew, and at last he went sea on a search of his own, spending five years roaming through Greece and Asia. At last, as he returned to Syracuse in despair, Aegeon concluded, he had come to Ephesus, "hopeless to find, yet loath to leave unsought … any place that harbors men."

When the ship sank, the floating mast struck a rock, separating the family.

Meanwhile, Antipholus and Dromio had arrived in Ephesus the same day as Aegeon. Antipholus, though, forewarned of the fatal restriction upon travelers from Syracuse, knew he must not reveal his true identity or origins. Moreover, neither Aegeon nor his Syracusan son and servant knew that the lost twins they sought lived in Ephesus! Also grown to manhood, they likewise went by the names Antipholus and Dromio!

Now Ephesus was a legendary land of magic, and its inhabitants purportedly practiced sorcery. Thus, when Antipholus of Syracuse encountered strangers in Ephesus who called him by name and seemed to know him, he attributed it to enchantment. Of course, he was being mistaken for his twin, Antipholus of Ephesus. Even Adriana, the wife of Antipholus of Ephesus, and her sister, Luciana, mistook the foreign Syracusan pair for their native Ephesian counterparts. Upon meeting Antipholus of Syracuse in town, Adriana insisted he come home for dinner. The puzzled Syracusan wondered aloud,

Even Adriana, the wife of Antipholus of Ephesus, and her sister, Luciana, mistook the Syracusan pair for their Ephesian counterparts.

"What, was I married to her in my dream? Or sleep I now and think I hear all this? What error drives our ears and eyes amiss?" To Dromio of Syracuse the explanation seemed obvious: "We talk with goblins, owls, and sprites; If we obey them not, this will ensue: They'll suck our breath, or pinch us black and blue."

Throughout the day the twin Antipholuses continued to be mistaken for one another by people of the city.

Nevertheless, the Syracusans eventually went home with Adriana. Unfortunately, Antipholus fell madly in love with Adriana's sister. When he confessed his adoration, however, Luciana implored the "unfaithful husband" to remain true to his wife.

Throughout the day, the twin Antipholuses continued to be mistaken for one another by people of the city. Yet, neither twin encountered the other, so each was left to speculate on the strange behavior of those around them. Antipholus of Syracuse prudently decided to flee the mystical city at the next possible opportunity. Antipholus of Ephesus, on the other hand, found the situation quite perplexing. He suddenly found himself greeted with allusions to earlier meetings of which he held no recollection; at dinnertime he found himself locked out of his house; at one point he was even arrested for not paying a debt that he had no memory of incurring. If this was a joke being perpetrated upon him, the Ephesian mused, it certainly was a most ingenious one!

The two Dromios felt equally bewildered. While on an errand for one Antipholus, either Dromio might be intercepted by the other Antipholus, who would demand the item that he had been sent to fetch – be it a loan of money, some repaired jewelry, a rope, or passage on a ship.

Inevitably, the baffled servant would be reprimanded for disobedience or insolence – or worse still, robbery.

The chaos peaked when Adriana attempted to have Antipholus of Ephesus, her own husband, along with his attendant, restrained and treated for lunacy. Complaints had raged from all quarters regarding the pair's wild behavior, forcing Adriana to conclude they were mad. She ordered them both bound and taken home, in hopes that there they might be cured.

Shortly after the two protesting Ephesians had been taken away, the visiting pair of Syracusians appeared on the street, rapiers drawn, attempting to flee Ephesus. When Adriana saw them, she thought that her husband and servant had escaped. While she summoned help to recapture them, the Syracusians took refuge in the abbey. The abbess, Aemilia, granted them sanctuary and denied their pursuers admittance to retrieve them.

By now, sunset approached, and with it, the hour assigned for Aegeon to meet his death. Solinus accompanied him to the site of execution. As they neared the gallows, Adriana appeared and begged the Duke to intervene and persuade the abbess to release the man she presumed to be her husband. Before Solinus could speak with the abbess, Antipholus of Ephesus arrived on the scene, newly escaped from his captors and thoroughly enraged at the ill-treatment he had received from his wife. Solinus attempted to settle the dispute, but each of the witnesses gave a different account of what had occurred. Stymied, Solinus wondered, "Why, what a strange impeach is this! I think you all have drunk of Circe's cup."

At this point, Aegeon recognized his long-lost son. When the abbess emerged from the abbey with the pair from Syracuse, the day's mysterious and confusing proceedings became clear. The long search at last was over. Not only had sons, father, and two sets of twins miraculously been restored to each other, but a married pair were reunited. The honorable abbess herself was the lost Aemilia – Aegeon's still-faithful wife! Solinus spared Aegeon's life and allowed the divided family to reunite. Adriana reconciled with her true husband, which left the Syracusan Antipholus free to court Luciana.

The chaos peaked when Adriana attempted to have Antipholus of Ephesus, her own husband … estrained and treated for lunacy.

And in the end, the two Dromios were still unable to distinguish between their masters, but it no longer mattered in the joy of reunion that swept over them all.

COMMENTARY

*T*he *Comedy of Errors*, unlike any other play Shakespeare wrote, contains no moralistic message, few memorable lines, and had little purpose other than entertaining its audience. Purely a farcical production, *The Comedy of Errors* is among Shakespeare's earliest works. We can detect elements that would reappear in his later works. Shakespeare returned to the motifs of identical twins and mistaken identity in *Twelfth Night*. This plot device grants the audience a comedic advantage over the characters by letting them in on a secret of which the characters are ignorant and upon which the plot turns. The audience's knowledge of the reason for the "errors" of identity that launch the comedy, offers them a privileged position from which it is comfortable to laugh, even as the characters fear for their sanity and safety.

Because the play stretches plausibility and believability to the extreme, critics characterize it as a farce, somewhat a blend of fantasy, improbability, charade and slapstick. No explanation is attempted, for instance, as to how the twins might have been so completely identical, even in habits of grooming and dress. Again, the realm of comedy allows the audience to grant the playwright such license in exchange for laughter. Nevertheless, we feel secure that the family will be reunited and the father will be spared execution. Indeed, it is safe to laugh when we are certain

The long search at last was over. Not only had sons, father, and two sets of twins miraculously been restored to each other, but a married pair were reunited.

there will be a happy ending. There is even a hint given that a wedding will soon take place between Antipholus of Syracuse and Luciana, a wedding being the standard conclusion of an Elizabethan comedic work.

Yet Shakespeare probes beyond mere farce in this comedy, exploring issues of a self that is left incomplete and isolated when deprived of its past and parentage. Thus, Antipholus of Syracuse pursues his lost kin with a yearning close to desperation:

> *I to the world am like a drop of water*
> *That in the ocean seeks another drop;*
> *Who, falling there to find his fellow forth,*
> *Unseen, inquisitive, confounds himself:*
> *So I, to find a mother and a brother,*
> *In quest of them, unhappy, lose myself.*

Only after finding his lost mother and brother is Antipholus of Syracuse able, as a whole being, to anticipate marriage and full adulthood.

The Two Gentlemen of Verona

TYPE OF WORK

Romantic comedy

SETTING

Italy

PRINCIPAL CHARACTERS

Proteus
A young gentleman of Verona

Valentine
His companion

Speed
The go-between for Proteus

Julia
*A young woman in love
with Proteus*

Silvia
*A young woman of Milan with
many suitors*

The Duke of Milan
Silvia's aristocratic father

Thurio
*A knight of Milan who hopes to
marry Silvia*

**Outlaws who live in exile
in the forest near Milan**

"Wilt thou be gone?" Proteus sadly asked his good friend Valentine. Although Valentine was indeed leaving for Milan, he had joyfully invited Proteus to accompany him. Proteus, however, had refused: he hoped to woo a girl in Verona named Julia.

Valentine considered his friend's pursuit to be foolish. "Love is your master," he scolded, "For he masters you." Would it not be infinitely more exciting to seek adventures abroad than to linger in Verona, "sluggardized" by infatuation?

But Proteus was intent on romance. So, bidding his friend farewell, he wished Valentine success and happiness in his studies in Milan. Once the student had departed, Proteus was left to wait for a response to the message he had sent to Julia.

Ironically, the go-between was a man named Speed; but to eager young Proteus, Speed seemed very slow indeed. When the messenger finally appeared, Proteus breathlessly inquired, "Gav'st thou my letter to Julia?" Speed conceded that he had, but he was not immediately inclined to discuss the particulars of his meeting with the girl; he only wanted to discuss the gratuity he expected for his services. Poor, impatient Proteus filled the man's hand with money, only to receive unwelcome news: Speed perceived Julia to be "hard as steel" in regards to Proteus.

Privately, however, Julia had rhapsodized over the young man's letter. While she did not choose to make a public show of her affections, Julia was deeply disposed to love him. Secretly she kissed Proteus's words, and sent him a letter of her own.

When Proteus received his beloved's letter, he was ecstatic to learn that she returned his love. But his joy soon turned to sorrow when his father demanded that Proteus go to Milan in order to gain experience through "travel in his youth." Meeting with Julia, Proteus promised to return to Verona as soon as possible. She slipped a ring on his finger and he promised to treasure it. In turn, he then gave Julia his ring, and bade her a wrenching farewell: "Alas, this parting strikes poor lovers dumb."

But even in his desolation, the heartsick lover remained an obedient son. Proteus dutifully set off for Milan. At least, he reflected, he would now enjoy the companionship of Valentine.

Surprisingly, the Valentine Proteus found in Milan bore little resemblance to the friend he had known in Verona. The cocksure young man who once scorned the mystery of love had become the love-smitten "puppet" of an exquisite girl named Silvia. So obsessed was Valentine with Silvia that he no longer had any inclination whatsoever to "discourse except it be of love."

Unfortunately for Valentine, Silvia's father, the Duke of Milan, still proposed that his daughter should marry Thurio, a noble-born but hopelessly shy and foolish knight. Recognizing Thurio as a fool, however, Valentine remained undaunted.

Meanwhile, Proteus himself had been quite charmed by Silvia on their first meeting. Thus he knew he had to praise the maid carefully, to avoid making his friend jealous.

Was not Sylvia "a heavenly saint"? asked Valentine. "No," Proteus finally answered. But she was, he allowed, "an earthly paragon." Disappointed with such a measured response, Valentine insisted that Proteus "call her divine." But Proteus held firm, saying, "I will not flatter her."

The cocksure young man who once scorned the mystery of love had become the love-smitten "puppet" of an exquisite girl named Silvia.

Nonetheless, as soon as he was alone, Proteus could not refrain from admitting to himself that Silvia was in fact "fair." As it turned out, Proteus was fickle and easily infatuated. "The remembrance of my former love," he marveled, "is by a newer object quite forgotten." Moreover, he had to admit that his loyalty to Valentine was now supplanted by his newfound devotion to the "perfections" of Sylvia. And Proteus decided that he would use his "skill" to win the girl.

Proteus's skill, sadly, took the form of treachery. Knowing that Valentine and Silvia planned to elope, Proteus visited the Duke and lost no time in detailing their scheme: Know noble lord, they have devised a mean

> *How he her chamber window will ascend*
> *And with a corded ladder fetch her down;*
> *For which the youthful lover now is gone....*

Thanking Proteus for alerting him to his daughter's plan, the Duke promised that he would not reveal Proteus's betrayal.

Shortly after Proteus left, Valentine arrived. Forewarned, the Duke searched Valentine's cloak, finding a ladder and a love letter written to Sylvia. "By heaven," the

Duke exploded, "my wrath shall far exceed the love I ever bore my daughter...." With that pronouncement, he banished Valentine from the city.

With Valentine out of the way, Proteus quickly devised a plot to trick the other rival for Silvia's affection, Thurio: First, he would lure the young nobleman to Silvia's house to sing her romantic, "wailful sonnets"; then, pretending to intervene on Thurio's behalf, Proteus would seize the occasion and proclaim his own love for Silvia. The poor, cowardly knight – who was well aware that Silvia detested him – readily agreed to take Proteus by his side when he went to court her.

The two gentlemen met beneath Silvia's window, as planned. After Thurio had serenaded his lady with a flowery, though fretful, love song, he hurried away, leaving Proteus to plead his cause to Silvia. And when Silvia appeared, Proteus took credit for the serenade and declared his own love for her. Silvia, though, was not pleased; she denounced Proteus for his broken faith with

"By heaven," the Duke exploded, "my wrath shall far exceed the love I ever bore my daughter...."

Julia, and called him a "false, perjured, disloyal man!"

> Julia watched from the shadows in horror as Proteus wooed Silvia.

"I grant, sweet love, that I did love a lady," Proteus persisted, desperately trying to win her. "But she is dead." Unbeknownst to either Proteus or Silvia, this lie devastated someone else who happened to be listening – Julia herself, Proteus's abandoned lady. Driven by the "fire of love," she had journeyed to Milan to visit her betrothed. Since it was not considered proper for young damsels to travel alone, she had even gone so far as to dress as a page. Still disguised in this garb, she watched from the shadows in horror as Proteus wooed Silvia.

Causing Julia even more pain, Proteus – who thought she was a boy named Sebastian – soon asked her to be his page. Then, to her chagrin, he instructed her to take a ring to Silvia – the very same ring that Julia had given Proteus before he had left Verona.

But Silvia would not accept the ring. Instead, she expressed compassion for the poor girl Proteus had left behind. In truth, Silvia was still in love with Valentine, and set off on a journey that day at sunset to find him. As soon as she had reached the forest outside Milan, however, she was accosted by outlaws. "O Valentine," Silvia cried, "this I endure for thee!"

The Duke, meanwhile, had learned that his daughter had "fled unto that peasant Valentine." Accompanied by Thurio, Proteus, and Julia – still disguised as a boy – he left Milan to find her.

The outlaws were about to carry the abducted Silvia to their captain's cave, when Proteus, who had rushed ahead of his companions, discovered her. Despite her circumstances, she was not relieved to see him. "I would have been a breakfast to the beast," she railed, "rather than have false Proteus rescue me." "I'll force thee to yield to my desire," he threatened.

Just at that moment, Valentine arrived. "Thou friend of an ill fashion!" he snarled at Proteus. He then launched into a tirade, elaborating all of his false friend's wrongdoings. Proteus listened quietly to Valentine, his words awakening old loyalties within his breast. Surprising everyone, he repented. "My shame and guilt confound me," he said, confessing remorse at his own treacherous acts. For his part, Valentine generously forgave Proteus: "And once again I do receive thee honest."

Overcome with emotion, the pageboy Julia swooned. When she awoke, she murmured, "My master charged me to deliver a ring to Madam Silvia, which of neglect was never done." Then she displayed the ring that Proteus had presented to her in Verona. "Julia!" Proteus exclaimed, at last recognizing her.

Julia gently chided him for his inconstancy, and, for the second time that day, Proteus felt remorse. Taking Julia's hand, he announced, "Bear witness heaven, I have my wish forever."

Meanwhile, nearby, the outlaws had captured the lagging Duke and Thurio. "A prize, a prize, a prize!" they shouted to their captain, rejoicing in their good fortune as they advanced toward the assembly. "Forbear, forbear I say," Valentine commanded the outlaws, finally revealing to his companions that he, in fact, was the outlaw captain. He explained that these were not wicked men, but simply "banished" citizens like himself. After listening carefully to Valentine, the Duke proclaimed, "Thou hast prevailed; I pardon them, and thee."

"I would have been a breakfast to the beast," she railed, "rather than have false Proteus rescue me."

All was forgiven – even Thurio had a change of heart about Silvia. "Sir Valentine," he stated boldly, "I care not for her."

And joy reigned triumphant in the forest when the Duke announced that the two couples would marry on that very day, and celebrate their "good devotion" ever after.

COMMENTARY

Written in the 1590s, *The Two Gentlemen of Verona* may have been Shakespeare's first comedy. Though it normally appears in his chronologies after *As You Like It* and *Twelfth Night*, many critics, noting shortcomings in the plot's structure, believe that *Two Gentlemen* precedes the other two comedies. In fact, it has been suggested that Shakespeare hurriedly wrote sections of the play in order to meet the deadline for a first performance.

While critics disagree about chronology, they tend to agree about the play's weaknesses. The final act is most frequently criticized: Proteus undergoes such a rapid and profound change in temperament that he seems to lose credibility as a character. One moment he denounces Valentine and is prepared to force himself on Valentine's fiancée; the next he begs Valentine's forgiveness – then proclaims his devotion to Julia rather than to the avidly-pursued Silvia. Although the name Proteus refers to a Greek sea-god who changes form, Shakespeare is nonetheless criticized for presenting his Proteus's chameleon nature only superficially, without motivation in the context of the play.

Whatever its shortcomings, *The Two Gentlemen of Verona* remains an important work. It is a seminal Shakespearean comedy that introduces themes and plot complications which resurface in later, more highly acclaimed plays. It is, for instance, the first play to use the ring-exchange, which also figures prominently in *All's Well That Ends Well*. Similarly, its use of the forest as a place of conflict resolution presages plays like *A Midsummer Night's Dream* and *As You Like It*. *The Two Gentlemen of Verona* is also the first of the comedies to employ a female character disguised as a male. Thus, while *Two Gentlemen* is by no means Shakespeare's most successful comedy, it still offers a unique glimpse into his development as a master playwright.

"Bear witness heaven, I have my wish forever."

The Winter's Tale

TYPE OF WORK

Tragicomic drama

SETTING

Sicily and Bohemia,
in the Golden Age

PRINCIPAL CHARACTERS

Polixenes
King of Bohemia

Leontes
King of Sicily

Hermione
Leontes' wife, the Queen of Sicily

Paulina
Her attendant

Camillo
Leontes' counselor

Perdita
*The daughter of Leontes
and Hermione*

Florizel
Polixenes' son

For nine months Polixenes, King of Bohemia, had been a guest at the court of his childhood friend Leontes, the King of Sicily. The time had come, however, when Polixenes – "question'd by fears" of what may "breed upon our absence" in Bohemia – made arrangements to return to his own palace.

L eontes, greatly distressed by his friend's parting, pleaded with him to stay "one seven-night longer." Still, Polixenes was determined to depart the next day. "Press me not, I beseech you," he replied.

Exasperated, Leontes turned to his wife Hermione. "Tongue-tied, our queen?" he said. "Speak you." Now Hermione, as it happened, was a woman of abundant charm and wit. Taking up her husband's cause, she cleverly argued that Polixenes could choose either to be her "prisoner" or her "guest."

"Your guest, then, madame," Polixenes finally relented. "Hermione, my dearest," Leontes said, complimenting his wife, "thou never spok'st to better purpose." Leontes had scarcely uttered these words, however, when a dark mood fell over him. Suddenly suspicious, he began to brood over the fact that Hermione had managed to persuade Polixenes to

Leontes, now that his jealousy was aroused, could not rid himself of the thought that he had been "much deceived."

stay another week, whereas he had failed. Perhaps, Leontes thought, she and Polixenes had made a "cuckold" of him; indeed, perchance the baby Hermione now carried was not his own.

Leontes, now that his jealousy was aroused, could not rid himself of the thought that he had been "much deceived." Unable to bear his suspicions alone any longer, he called for his trusted counselor Camillo. "How I am galled," Leontes raged, denouncing Hermione as "rank" and Polixenes as his "enemy." But Camillo, being most wise, tried to calm his lord. Leontes was imagining these things; his wife would never betray him for another. Leontes, however, could not be pacified – and ordered Camillo to "bespice a cup" of Polixenes' wine with enough poison to give his old friend "a lasting wink."

Camillo, wishing only to placate Leontes, agreed to carry out the plan and then left. Shortly afterwards, he ran into Polixenes, who, having noted Leontes' disturbed countenance, pressed Camillo for an explanation, whereupon Camillo revealed Leontes' plan to poison him. Incredulous, Polixenes wondered aloud how such an infectious jealousy could take root in his friend. "I know not," Camillo answered, but one thing was certain: they

Not long after her imprisonment, Hermione gave birth to a baby girl.

should both make their escape to Bohemia that very night.

When Leontes learned the next day that Polixenes and Camillo had taken flight, he became further enraged. Venting his fury on Hermione, he publicly denounced her as "an adulteress," separated her from their young son Mamillus, and then imprisoned her.

Although many of the court protested Hermione's treatment, Leontes, could not be pacified – and ordered Camillo to "bespice a cup" of Polixenes' wine with enough poison to give his old friend "a lasting wink."

proclaiming her innocence, Leontes, now entirely mad, insisted that it was Polixenes who had made his wife pregnant – who had made her "swell thus."

Not long after her imprisonment, Hermione gave birth to a baby girl. Confident that Leontes would "soften at the sight of the child," Hermione's attendant Paulina brought the infant to the King. But Leontes' wrath only intensified. "Take up the bastard," he roared. "The bastard's brains with these my proper hands shall I dash out." Paulina, stunned by the King's reaction, shielded the infant from his wrath. Seeing that his servants were sympathetic toward the child, Leontes commanded Paulina's husband Antigonus to take it from the kingdom and abandon it in "some remote desert place [where] chance might nurse or end it." This Antigonus performed. Leontes then announced that the Delphic Oracle would be consulted to settle the matter of Hermione's guilt.

Aware that his palace lords were also sympathetic to Hermione, Leontes decided to grant her a public trial. Hermione, standing before the court, steadfastly maintained her innocence. Then, in the midst of the trial, messengers arrived with Apollo's "seal'd-up oracle" from Delphi. Everyone listened intently as its contents were read:

... the Delphic Oracle would be consulted to settle the matter of Hermione's guilt.

Hermione is chaste; Polixenes, blameless; Camillo, a true subject; Leontes, a jealous tyrant; his innocent babe, truly begotten; and the king shall live without an heir if that which is lost not be found.

"There is no truth at all i' the oracle," Leontes protested. Barely a moment later, however, he was brought news that his beloved son Mamillus had died. "Apollo is angry," the grief-stricken Leontes cried, suddenly aware that the oracle was indeed coming to pass.

Devastated at hearing of Mamillus' death, Hermione collapsed. "The news is mortal to the queen," Paulina lamented, as Leontes mourned the tragic losses of both his son and his wife.

Sixteen years passed. During that time, the repentant Leontes had thought only of Mamillus, Hermione, and the lost "poor babe." But Perdita, as the child became known, had not in fact died. Forsaken by Antigonus on the coast of Bohemia with a bundle of gold and jewels, she had been found by a kindly shepherd and raised as his daughter. Now "grown in grace," the beautiful Perdita was being wooed by Florizel, the Prince of Bohemia and heir to its throne.

Florizel, Polixenes's only son, could think of nothing but "the celebration of that nuptial" which would unite him eternally to his beloved Perdita. As a result, he had recently neglected his duties at court, a point which had not escaped his father's notice. Moreover, although Polixenes had not met Perdita, he objected in principle to his son's courting a girl of such humble origins.

One night, to learn more about Perdita, he decided to pay her a visit.

Dressed in disguises, Polixenes and his trusted friend Camillo – who had settled in Bohemia after fleeing Leontes' services – arrived at the shepherd's cottage during sheep-shearing, an annual celebration. To his chagrin, Polixenes not only found Florizel there, but he also overheard him propose marriage to Perdita.

"Make your divorce, young sir," countered the angry Polixenes, removing his disguise. "For thee, fond boy," he continued, "we'll bar thee from succession." Florizel was angry, but, at the same time, torn. He knew Polixenes would disown him if he wed lowly Perdita, and yet he could not forget her. Choosing to obey "fancy" instead of his father, Florizel decided to elope with Perdita and escape to a foreign country. Camillo, who was sympathetic to the pair, suggested they sail for Sicily. Once there, he

"Apollo is angry," the grief-stricken Leontes cried, suddenly aware that the oracle was indeed coming to pass.

advised them, Florizel could present himself to Leontes as an emissary from Bohemia, and, following Camillo's instructions to the letter, win Leontes' favor.

Meanwhile, Perdita's adopted father had decided that the only way he could escape the King's ire was to tell him the story of how he had found Perdita and the gold. On his way to Polixenes' palace, however, the shepherd was waylaid by a rogue and taken aboard Florizel's ship.

When Florizel and Perdita arrived in Sicily, Leontes informed them they were as welcome at his court "as is the spring to the earth." Polixenes, though, who was yet determined to stop Florizel's marriage to Perdita, soon followed and denounced his son to Leontes and his court.

The shepherd, seizing Polixenes' arrival as a final opportunity to save himself, then related the story of his adopted daughter's abandonment, and presented Polixenes and Leontes with his evidence: the bundled gold and jewels. The old kings were stunned; Leontes, overcome with joy, announced, "Our Perdita is found." And though this joy was compounded by his reunion with Polixenes and Camillo, he nonetheless lamented that Hermione was not there to share his happiness.

Leontes, overcome with joy, announced, "Our Perdita is found."

One day, Paulina, ever loyal to her mistress's memory, invited Leontes, his friends, and his new family to view a newly-fashioned statue of the Queen. When she opened a curtain to reveal the lifelike sculpture, Leontes marveled at the "air that comes from her" and wondered aloud at what "fine chisel could ever yet cut breath."

Choosing to obey "fancy" instead of his father, Florizel decided to elope with Perdita …

No longer able to restrain himself, Leontes approached the statue to kiss its lips. Just then, Paulina mysteriously issued her command: "Music, activate her!" To everyone's surprise and delight, Hermione, who was "stone no more," descended from the pedestal.

"O! she's warm," Leontes cried out. After having lived in seclusion for so many years, dreaming only that Perdita might be found, Hermione now fell joyously into the arms of her long-lost daughter and her contrite husband.

COMMENTARY

*T*he *Winter's Tale* was one of Shakespeare's late plays (approx. 1611). While he undoubtedly borrowed many elements of plot from Robert Greene's romance *Pandosto: The Triumph of Time* (1588), Shakespeare made several changes, including, most notably, the ultimate fate of Hermione.

The Winter's Tale has had an odd history in Shakespeare's canon. Frequently regarded as an imperfect work – a work marred by an uncharacteristically bleak and fanciful vision of nature and culture – the play now enjoys a reputation as being among Shakespeare's best and most imaginative works.

In part, the play's anomalous reputation can be explained by the fact that it represents a departure of sorts, both in terms of dramatic substance and techniques. Thus, for instance, although Shakespeare's work manifested a lifelong interest in mythology and folklore, *The Winter's Tale* takes that interest in a new direction, employing folkloric and mythological material in an episodic narrative that one critic has characterized as filled with "wild improbabilities" and "arbitrary symbolism."

Moreover, unlike many earlier works, this play brings these fantastic improbabilities to center stage and makes "fancy" its central theme. The effect is that both the drama and the narrative challenge our notions of nature and culture, particularly as these ideas relate to "generation." By drawing attention, then, to the "staged" or fictive elements of nature and culture, Shakespeare perhaps reminds us that generation – at least in the artistic sense of the word – is a process of constructing what is "natural" to us, or – as in the case of Perdita – recovering what is lost to us.

In this respect, *The Winter's Tale* – though it plays on traditional associations with a "sad tale" – may be one of Shakespeare's more benevolent visions of the fate of our nature and our culture.

No longer able to restrain himself, Leontes approached the statue to kiss its lips.

SHAKESPEARE AT A GLANCE

COMEDIES

TRAGEDIES

HISTORIES

"How sharper that a serpent's tooth it is To have a thankless child!"

King Lear

… As the queen fell to the ground, crying,
"The drink, the drink!
I am poison'd!" Hamlet demanded that
the treachery be revealed.

Hamlet

"Beware the Ides of March."

Julius Caesar

"O, she doth teach the torches to burn bright.... Did my heart love till now?"

Romeo and Juliet

As Macbeth was preparing for war, his wife, chafing under her own guilty conscience, was walking in her sleep, attempting to wash from her hands invisible bloodstains.

Macbeth

"... Then must you speak of one that lov'd not wisely but too well.... Of one whose hand ... threw a pearl away."

Othello

Hamlet, Prince of Denmark

TYPE OF WORK

Tragic drama

SETTING

Elsinore, Denmark;
c. 1200

PRINCIPAL CHARACTERS

Hamlet
*Prince of Denmark and son of the
former king*

The Ghost
Hamlet's dead father

Gertrude
*Hamlet's mother, and
Queen of Denmark*

Claudius
*Hamlet's uncle and new stepfather,
and now, King of Denmark*

Polonius
Claudius's chief counselor

Laertes
Polonius's son

Ophelia
Polonius's obedient daughter

Horatio
Hamlet's faithful friend

Prince Hamlet bitterly opposed the marriage of his mother, Gertrude, to Claudius, her own brother-in-law, so soon after her husband's death. Moreover, Hamlet had a strange suspicion that the new king – his stepfather and former uncle – had somehow plotted his father's mysterious demise, and he refused to cease mourning his natural father, now two months dead.

As Hamlet languished in resentfulness, he was approached by his close friend Horatio, who revealed that for three nights now castle guards had seen the former king stalking the parapets – as a ghost. He persuaded the prince that his father must have some message of importance to impart, and thus Hamlet should wait with him that night for the ghost to appear again.

The bloody apparition was indeed the image of Hamlet's father. In horror, the son listened with Horatio as the dead king described how his brother Claudius had seduced Gertrude, and how the two of them together had arranged for his murder, while claiming that a serpent had injected the fatal poison.

Hamlet was appalled – though not entirely surprised – at this revelation. But he was even more shaken when the ghost made a desperate plea: he

… he was even more shaken when the ghost made a desperate plea: he ordered Hamlet to avenge his death by killing Claudius …

ordered Hamlet to avenge his death by killing Claudius, but cautioned that Gertrude must be spared; heaven alone should punish her for her sins.

Now, Hamlet considered himself an intellectual, not a soldier or a man of action. This charge to exact revenge posed a real dilemma in the prince's mind. He swore Horatio to secrecy concerning the ghost and continued for the next few days to fret on what he must do.

Filled with suppressed anger toward both his mother and Claudius, and torn between doing his duty in honor and carrying out a most distasteful and bloody task, Hamlet began to act more and more erratic. Ophelia, his lady friend and the daughter of the new king's most trusted counselor, Polonius, reported Hamlet's eccentric behavior to her father. Polonius insisted that Hamlet had become demented, and cautioned Ophelia to keep her distance. He then reported Hamlet's bizarre turn to the king and queen.

Perceiving Hamlet as a possible threat to the throne, Claudius, Gertrude and Polonius hired two dull-witted courtiers, Rosencrantz and Guildenstern, to spy on the prince, to learn whether he in fact coveted their power or was merely mad. But Hamlet, within minutes, recognized the charade and the motives behind it, and caustically mocked them. And shortly, it seemed to Hamlet that everyone – including Ophelia – was acting as a spy and an informant for King Claudius and Queen Gertrude.

By now the prince was dashed by doubts and worries. He began to wonder if his father's ghost had really appeared; maybe it had been a vision from the devil instead. After all, the thought of murdering Claudius, vile and hated though he was, still repelled Hamlet. But soon he struck upon an idea: a company of traveling actors was visiting Elsinore, and Hamlet persuaded them to perform a murder scene that was actually a reenactment of the death of the old king. He was sure that if Claudius and Gertrude had in fact killed his father, their guilt would play on their faces and show in their actions.

The play proceeded. Sure enough, Claudius became so unnerved both by the drama and by Hamlet's sly, taunting comments that he stormed from the performance, with Gertrude close behind.

Gertrude sent posthaste for her insolent son. When he visited her in her room to discuss the matter, Polonius was secreted behind a curtain, listening. Soon the exchange between mother and son grew more heated and violent. When Polonius cried out for the guards, Hamlet, thinking he was Claudius, stabbed through the curtain and killed him. Amid this confusion, the ghost of Hamlet's father once more appeared (invisible to Gertrude) and again reminded his son of his original commission: to kill Claudius.

With renewed determination, Hamlet gripped his dagger and made for Claudius's bedchamber. But when he entered the room, prepared at last to do the deed, he found

Now, Hamlet considered himself an intellectual, not a soldier or a man of action.

Claudius praying. This sight utterly undid the prince's resolve; he could not slay this man while in the posture of supplication to God, as a prayerful soul, he reasoned, would be swept straight to heaven – and Claudius deserved nothing higher than hell. So, the prince once again delayed his revenge.

Now Claudius, seeing the danger he was in, ordered that Hamlet be hurried off to England on the next possible ship. Again, Rozencrantz and Guildenstern were commissioned to carry out this clandestine errand, which secretly included orders for the murder of the prince on his arrival.

Several days before Hamlet was taken aboard ship, he witnessed a conquering Norwegian army marching past en route to a distant battle. Their leader-captain was young

… torn between doing his duty in honor and carrying out a most distasteful and bloody task, Hamlet began to act more and more erratic.

Fortinbras, whose father had once lost many skirmishes and much property to Hamlet's own father. In harmony with his threats to invade Denmark to avenge these losses, Fortinbras, "a delicate and tender prince," was now dutifully acting on his father's wishes. Hamlet felt ashamed that he lacked equal willpower and character in response to filial duty.

As Hamlet was departing for England, Laertes, Polonius's hot-tempered son, arrived from Paris, seeking his own revenge. Enraged that Ophelia, his own sister, would allow Hamlet to escape unpunished, he lashed into her. Ophelia, now rejected by her banished lover and driven to madness by feelings of guilt borrowed from an embittered brother, drowned herself.

Hamlet, sensing a plot against his life, had altered his guards' orders: Rosencrantz and Guildenstern, not he, were killed by assassins on touching English soil. The prince then sent word back to Denmark that he had been captured by pirates and would soon be returning to his home.

Claudius was dismayed to learn that his plans to do away with his pesky stepson had gone awry. So, together with Laertes, he hatched a new line of attack: Laertes would challenge Hamlet to a duel and kill him with a poison-tipped foil. If the fencing match failed to do the trick, a poison-spiked drink would be in easy reach of the dueler. One way or another, meddling Prince Hamlet would be no more.

Upon Hamlet's return, he and Horatio stood in a churchyard, discussing the prince's perilous journey. In the distance they spied a funeral procession. The two concealed themselves and looked on at the passage of Ophelia's funeral train, led by Laertes, pompously bewailing his dead sister. Unable to endure such a false and pretentious display, Hamlet leapt out of hiding and lunged toward Laertes. Both men were restrained, but not until after the challenge to duel was made – and accepted.

To diminish suspicion that he was in any way involved with the plot, King Claudius bet heavily on the practiced swordsman Hamlet. Then, according to plan, poison was dripped onto Laertes' rapier and into the convenient cup.

But things soon began to miscarry. First, the unsuspecting Gertrude raised and drank from the spiked cup in a toast to her son. In the contest that followed, Laertes wounded Hamlet, and Hamlet in turn fatally pierced Laertes. Then, as the queen fell to the ground, crying, "The drink, the drink! I am poison'd!" Hamlet demanded that the treachery be revealed. At this, dying Laertes spoke up and exposed the plot – the poisoned wine and the venom-tipped foil, whose effects Hamlet would soon feel. Laertes further divulged that "the King's to blame": Claudius had authored the entire miserable scene.

Hesitating no longer, Hamlet rushed forward, drove his sword's blade through Claudius, and cursed the "incestuous, murderous, damn'd Dane." Then Laertes and Hamlet turned and implored each other's forgiveness, that

Hamlet gripped his dagger and made for Claudius's bedchamber.

Hesitating no longer, Hamlet rushed forward, stabbed Claudius, and cursed the "incestuous, murderous, damn'd Dane."

they might both die in peace. Within minutes, Fortinbras arrived, and, with Hamlet's dying approval, appropriated the throne of Denmark – a throne so tragically twice vacated in the previous few months.

COMMENTARY

What can be said about the most famous work of English drama? A lot, actually. In fact scholars have been pawing over this play for some 400 years, searching to explain the inner workings of its plot, and particularly debating why the intelligent young Hamlet had such a hard time mustering the courage to avenge his father's death. Often the only thing these scholars agree upon is that Hamlet's speeches and mannerisms are complex, allusive, and sometimes cryptic.

One thing is certain: Hamlet follows the conventions of a standard Elizabethan genre – the "revenge play" – of which there are many examples. But Shakespeare's poetic drama is by far more expansive and more ambiguous than any of these other works.

It has been suggested that the prince's delayed revenge, as opposed to Fortinbras' decisiveness, is meant to contrast two universal individuals: the man of contemplation and the man of action. The university-bred Hamlet analyzes everything too deeply and is thus prevented from taking any clear course:

> ... *Thinking too precisely on the event*
> *a thought which, quartered, hath but one part wisdom*
> *and ever three parts coward, I do not know*

why, yet I live to say "this thing's to do,"
sith I have cause and will and strength and means to do't.

But Hamlet's essential dilemma is one that has confronted mankind throughout the ages; and this confrontation – between duty and morality, courage and fear, right and wrong – will assuredly persist for all ages to come.

One way or another, meddling Prince Hamlet would be no more.

King Lear

TYPE OF WORK

Tragic drama

SETTING

Medieval England

PRINCIPAL CHARACTERS

Lear
King of Britain

Cordelia
His faithful daughter

Regan and Goneril
His two mean-spirited daughters

The Dukes of Cornwall and Albany
Their husbands

The Earl of Gloucester Edmund
The Earl's treacherous son

Edgar
The Earl's true son (later disguised as a madman)

The Duke of Kent
Cordelia's loyal helper

Lear's Fool
A comical character

England's aged King Lear had chosen to renounce his throne and divide the kingdom among his three daughters. He promised the greatest portion of the empire to whichever daughter proved to love him most. Goneril lavished exaggerated praise on her father; Regan even outdid her sister with a wordy show of hollow affection. Cordelia, however, refused to stoop to flattery, and insisted that she loved her father no more and no less than was his due. Lear exploded at what seemed to him her lack of tenderness and promptly disowned her. Moreover, Lear banished the Duke of Kent from the castle for defending Cordelia.

Two suitors had come to the British court to seek Cordelia's hand: the Duke of Burgundy and the King of France. After Lear had disinherited Cordelia, Burgundy suddenly lost interest in her – he aspired to a wealthy bride. The King of France, on the other hand, was delighted by Cordelia's honesty and immediately asked for her hand. They departed for France, without Lear's blessing, and Cordelia's part of the kingdom was divided between Goneril and Regan, who were all too happy at their sister's fall from grace. Furthermore, these two daughters decided that Lear had succumbed to a sort of senility, and they set upon a

Cordelia insisted that she loved her father no more and no less than was his due.

strategy to exploit his weakness to their own advantage.

Meanwhile, in the Earl of Gloucester's castle, Edmund, Gloucester's bitter and cunning illegitimate son, was fretting over his father's preference toward the legitimate brother, Edgar. Edmund now forged a letter in which Edgar supposedly expressed his intent to murder their father. Gloucester straightway accepted the letter as true and fled in distress from the palace. Then Edmund, in mock concern, went and warned his brother that someone had turned Gloucester against him. Edgar, too good at heart to suspect his brother's treachery, believed the story and escaped to the forest. Thus, in two clever strokes Edmund had managed to supplant his brother in his father's affections.

After dividing his kingdom, Lear decided to lodge for a time at Goneril's palace. Now that she had her half of his kingdom, however, she no longer feigned love for him. In fact, she so disdained her father that she ordered her servants to mistreat and insult him. Accordingly, her servants began to deal with him as a doddering old man rather than as a king.

In the meantime, the banished Duke of Kent, now in disguise, presented himself to the king at Goneril's palace. Lear failed to recognize the disguise and hired Kent as a servant. Then, with the help of the King's Fool (whose biting jibes and puns provide some of the finest moments in all literature), Kent began hinting to Lear that he had acted unwisely in dealing with Cordelia, until the King began to perceive his folly. As Goneril continued to humiliate him, Lear, bemoaning his fate ("How sharper than a serpent's tooth it is/To have a thankless child!"),

> Goneril ...
> so distained
> her father that
> she ordered her
> servants to
> mistreat and
> insult him.

determined to move on to Regan's household. He did not know that Regan was at that moment on her way to visit Gloucester. (In fact, all of the characters were now converging on Gloucester's castle).

Near Gloucester, Edgar, still convinced that his life was in peril from his father, lingered in a local wood, disguised as a madman – Tom o' Bedlam.

Soon Regan and her husband, the Duke of Cornwall, arrived at Gloucester. They were followed by King Lear not long after. When Goneril and her household also appeared, the two sisters united to disgrace their father, ordering him to dismiss all his servants. But this embarrassment proved too much for the old King, who, in a fit of anger and shame, rushed out of the castle into a furious storm, where he wandered about madly, screaming and cursing. Their plan having succeeded, the daughters locked the doors behind him. (Then follows a most famous and stirring scene: With Kent looking on in disbelief, Lear rages and curses in the midnight storm, with his frightened Fool cowering beside him, uttering the most biting and ironic jokes.)

Fortunately, Gloucester found the wretched twosome and led them to a little hovel, where they encountered

"How sharper than a serpent's tooth it is/ To have a thankless child!"

Lear, now half mad himself, set about conducting a bizarre mock trial of his daughters ...

Edgar, still masquerading as the deranged Tom o'Bedlam. Lear, now half mad himself, set about conducting a bizarre mock trial of his daughters, with Kent, the Fool and Edgar all serving in his "court." (The mixture of Lear's denunciations, Edgar's incoherent chatter, the Fool's punning and ironic commentary, and Kent's astonished silence, create a superb scene of absurdity and despair.)

Meanwhile, Kent had heard that Cordelia, back in France, was preparing to ship a small army across the English Channel to rescue Lear. But Edmund, who had also got wind of this news, hinted to Regan's husband, the Duke of Cornwall, that Gloucester planned to side with Lear and the French army against Regan and Goneril. Cornwall was furious, and agreed to avenge himself on innocent Gloucester. (Very convenient for Edmund, of course, as he would inherit his father's earldom!)

It was now a race against time: could Gloucester, Edgar, Kent and Lear hold out against the treachery of Edmund, Regan, Goneril and Cornwall until help arrived from France? They devised a plan to flee to Dover, there to await the coming of Cordelia and the French troops. King Lear managed to make his escape in time, drawn by Kent in a litter, but Gloucester was not so lucky – Cornwall caught

"'Tis the time's plague when madmen lead the blind."

him, jabbed out both his eyes, then thrust him through the castle gates to "let him smell his way to Dover." Crawling about blindly, the Earl bumped into none other than his own son, Edgar, still pretending to be insane. Edgar agreed to lead his father – who remained unapprised of his true identity – to Dover, though and Gloucester bitterly complained: "Tis the time's plague when madmen lead the blind."

While Kent with Lear and Edgar with Gloucester were making their separate ways to Dover, a love affair brewed among the villains. Goneril had become infatuated with the diabolical Edmund, who returned with her to her palace. There she fell into a bitter argument with her husband, the Duke of Albany, who vehemently chastised Goneril for her mistreatment of Lear. Albany also informed his wife that Cornwall had been killed, struck down by one of Gloucester's servants. Suddenly a frightening thought paralyzed Goneril: now that her sister was a widow, would she too pursue Edmund and his rising star? This fear was soon confirmed when Regan sent a message to the castle professing her love for Edmund,

He assured his father that he had seen him fall from the dizzy height and survive – he'd seen a miracle!

followed by an invitation to join forces with her.
Since Albany's sympathies were now with Lear, Goneril
was forced to watch in frustrated rage as her sister and
Edmund set out together with their cohorts against the
expected invasion.

In the meantime, at Dover, Kent met with the French
officials while Cordelia sent doctors to treat her father,
who, by that time, was mentally and physically spent.
But Lear refused to meet with Cordelia; he had come to
understand his injuries against his loyal daughter and now
felt too ashamed to see her.

On his journey to Dover, the blind Gloucester had
grown more and more distressed. At last he implored
Edgar to guide him to the brink of a cliff so that he could
throw himself off. But Edgar fooled him into thinking the
level ground was actually the top of a ridge. And when
Gloucester fell forward onto the ground, as if leaping from
a cliff, Edgar changed his voice, pretending to be a passerby
at the cliff's base. He assured his father that he had seen
him fall from the dizzy height and survive – he'd seen
a miracle! Gloucester believed the tale and accepted the
"miracle" as a sign that he was meant to live.

Now Lear, who had been delirious before he was finally
rescued by Cordelia, fell into a deep sleep. On awakening,
he found himself purged of his madness, and begged
Cordelia's forgiveness. Their reconciliation complete, they
were ready to join with Kent and the French army against
Edmund and his forces. But Cordelia's troops were
defeated, and Edmund sent orders that Lear and his
daughter be executed.

Meanwhile, Regan had collapsed in death, poisoned by
her own jealous sister. (Goneril herself would later die by
suicide.) Just at that moment, Edgar burst in on the scene,

engaged his brother Edmund in combat, and dealt him
a mortal wound. He then cast off his disguise and revealed
his true identity to his dying brother, also reporting that
Gloucester, their father, had died a few hours before.
Edmund, apparently touched by the news of his father's
death, confessed that he had ordered the executions of Lear
and Cordelia, and dispatched a messenger to stop them.

It was, alas, too late. Lear entered, carrying the body
of his beloved daughter, then he too fell and died,
brokenhearted. Only Albany, Kent and Edgar survived.
It fell to these last two to jointly rule the shattered nation.

COMMENTARY

Since *King Lear's* setting is pre-Christian Britain,
some readers chafe under the sort of nihilistic fatalism that
colors the characters' thinking ("As flies to wanton boys we
are to the gods...."). And in fact, it's hard to think of any
other play so vast, passionate and bitter as this. The work
is unusually demanding on the reader or spectator, with so
many prominent figures suffering so much for so long,
only, in the end, to find so little redemption.

True, there is a good deal of humor throughout the play,
especially in the lightning-fast wisecracks and puns of
the Fool and in the cryptic babble of Edgar masquerading
as a madman. But even the humor has a steady, grim
undertone.

The main plot is marvelously conceived. Just as Lear
mistakenly believes that Cordelia has wronged him and his
other daughters have served him, so Gloucester jumps
to the conclusion that Edgar opposes him and Edmund

defends him – when in both cases precisely the opposite is true. The horrific consequences of these misjudgments intertwine and drive the action along.

On awakening, he found himself purged of his madness and begged Cordelia's forgiveness.

Romeo and Juliet

TYPE OF WORK

Romantic tragedy

SETTING

Verona, Italy;
Fifteenth century

PRINCIPAL CHARACTERS

Romeo
Son of the house of Montague

Juliet
Daughter of the Capulet household

Benvolio
Romeo's cousin

Mercutio
Romeo's friend

Tybalt
Juliet's cousin

Lady Montague
The clan's matriarch

Lady Capulet
Juliet's mother

Juliet's ribald nurse

Friar Lawrence
A Franciscan Monk

For a very long time the Capulets and the Montagues had been feuding. Harsh words often led to violence between the two houses, who were sworn as deadly enemies. Prince Escalus of Verona happened upon one such bloody brawl and angrily pronounced, "If ever you disturb our streets again, your lives shall pay the forfeit of the peace."

Shortly after this, Romeo and his cousin Benvolio met on the street, and Romeo sadly confessed his unrequited love for an aloof and indifferent young woman. "[Give] liberty unto thine eyes; Examine other beauties," was Benvolio's curative. But Romeo was unmoved: "Thou canst not teach me to forget."

Meanwhile, as Lord Capulet arranged for the marriage of Juliet, his 14-year-old daughter, to Paris, a kinsman of the Prince, he advised Paris to woo the girl gently. That night Capulet was to give a party so Paris could meet Juliet. He called a servant to deliver the invitations.

Now the servant could not read, so as he walked along he petitioned Romeo and Benvolio to read the guest list to him. In thanks, he told Romeo, "If you be not of the house of Montagues, I pray come and crush a cup a wine." Since Romeo's unreceptive Rosaline was named among the guests, Benvolio urged Romeo to go and find out for himself that Rosaline was a "crow."

As Romeo and his friend Mercutio, both wearing masks, searched for Rosaline among the gathering,

Romeo's eyes fell upon the exquisite Juliet –
and Romeo remembered Rosaline no more.
"O, she doth teach the torches to burn bright!…
Did my heart love till now?" he chimed. However,
fiery Tybalt, Capulet's nephew, overheard
Romeo pouring out his heart and reported to his
uncle that a Montague had invaded their festivity.
But Capulet was not alarmed and would have no
bloodshed; besides, Romeo seemed to be "a virtuous and
well-governed youth."

Romeo approached Juliet offering "my lips, two
blushing pilgrims," to which Juliet replied, "Ay, pilgrim,
lips that thou must use in prayer." But Romeo at last
convinced her to press her lips to his – just before Juliet's
Capulet mother called her away. Romeo was stunned by
this revelation that the girl was a daughter of his father's
enemy, but vowed that not even death would keep him
from his true love.

The party ended, leaving Romeo outside the Capulet
house, gazing up in lovesick rapture at Juliet's window.
Just then, to his joy, Juliet leaned from her balcony. Romeo
whispered: "But soft! What light through yonder window
breaks? It is the East, and Juliet is the sun!" As he debated
within himself whether to speak to her, she, thinking
herself alone, began to pour out her heart: "O Romeo,
Romeo! wherefore art thou Romeo? Deny thy father and
refuse thy name; or, if thou wilt not, be but sworn my love,
and I'll no longer be a Capulet."

Unable to contain himself, Romeo stepped out of the
shadows. Though ashamed at her overheard declaration,
Juliet reconfirmed her passion, but warned him that if her
family discovered him there, he would be killed. Romeo
was not alarmed, "For stony limits cannot hold love out."

Romeo's eyes
fell upon the
exquisite Juliet
– and Romeo
remembered
Rosaline no
more …

As he swore of his love by the moon, and by his heart, Juliet begged him not to swear at all. Things were happening too fast; the world seemed suddenly brilliant and fragile "like the lightening which doth cease to be." So, the fragile lovers exchanged vows and agreed to meet the next morning.

On his way home, Romeo stopped by the monastery to visit Friar Lawrence. "Our Romeo hath not been in bed tonight," the Franciscan observed. "I have been feasting with mine enemy," replied the young man. "... Plainly know my heart's dear love is set on the fair daughter of rich Capulet ... what thou must combine by holy marriage." The Friar teased Romeo for his fickle nature (only yesterday he had professed undying love for Rosaline), but agreed to perform the marriage, in the hope that "this alliance may so happy prove to turn your households' rancor to pure love."

The following morning, Mercutio and Benvolio were worriedly searching for Romeo; Tybalt had sent out a challenge for him to fight. But when the pair finally met up with their enamored young kinsman, he was in no mood

"But soft! What light through yonder window breaks? It is the East, and Juliet is the sun!"

for fighting. At this point Juliet's nurse came on the scene and took Romeo aside to demand his intentions. Romeo assured her that his love was in earnest and bade her bring Juliet to the Friar's cell, where they would be married that afternoon.

The wedding was performed; the lovers were to again meet later that evening. But that afternoon Benvolio and Mercutio ran into Tybalt and some of his men. Though Benvolio, remembering the Prince's edict, declined to duel, Mercutio and Tybalt began a joust of insults, with Mercutio's wit outdoing the other's words. Just then, the newly-married Romeo appeared, and Tybalt demanded that the "villain" fight. Romeo protested, "I never injured thee, but love thee better than thou canst devise." Mercutio, however, ached for a skirmish, and he and the equally hot-tempered Tybalt drew their sabers. Romeo stepped between the two, but Tybalt thrust forward and stabbed Mercutio, then bolted away. As the dying Mercutio was carried off, Romeo, torn with anger and mixed loyalties, confronted and killed Tybalt. Benvolio then implored his cousin to hide in order to avoid revenge or arrest.

> Romeo protested, "I never injured thee, but love thee better than thou canst devise."

"O Romeo, Romeo! wherefore art thou Romeo? Deny thy father and refuse thy name; or, if thou wilt not, be but sworn my love, and I'll no longer be a Capulet."

The Prince and a group of citizens came upon the bloody scene and called for an explanation from Benvolio. Silencing arguments as to where the blame fell, the Prince declared, "I will be deaf to pleading and excuses. When Romeo is found he shall be put to death."

Juliet impatiently awaited the arrival of her husband, when her nurse came with the news: "Tybalt is gone, and ... Romeo that killed him, he is banished." Distraught, Juliet sent the nurse off once again: "O, find him! give this ring to my true knight."

The Friar had a plan: He gave her a vial with a potion inside that would make her appear to be dead ...

In the meantime, Romeo, hidden in the Friar's cell, had just been informed of a change of heart by the Prince – rather than death, Romeo should only be exiled from Verona. Then the nurse came with news from Juliet: "She weeps and weeps." The Friar advised Romeo to wait until nightfall and then go to his true love.

That night Romeo went to Juliet's room; as dawn broke, the lovers could barely let themselves part. Soon after, Lady Capulet entered Juliet's chamber, believing the girl had stayed secreted in mourning for Tybalt. She spoke of the murder and the vengeance it demanded. "But now," she announced at last, "I'll tell thee joyful tidings, girl"; and she apprised her daughter that she would soon be married to Paris. When Juliet balked at any such wedding, her father flared up in anger: "I tell thee what – get thee to church ... or never after look me in the face."

Juliet now hurried to the Friar's cell, both to confess her filial disobedience and to see Romeo. There she met Paris, who was arranging for their forthcoming marriage. Though Juliet openly confessed to loving another, Paris mistook her words as a declaration towards him and promised that they would be married in bliss. After he left,

Juliet turned to Friar Lawrence for help. Indeed, the Monk had a plan: He gave her a vial with a potion inside that would make her appear to be dead, but in reality would only bring on a long sleep. When her family discovered her "lifeless" body, they would place it in the Capulets' tomb, and the Friar would then send for Romeo to rescue her and take her away from Verona.

The Capulets rejoiced when Juliet returned home and told her family that she would consent to marry Paris. But on the evening before the wedding, Juliet partook of the potion, and the next morning, when the Friar and Paris came to seek the bride, they found the parents filled with grief. They took Juliet's limp body, according to plan, to the family tomb.

Meanwhile, in Mantua, word of Juliet's death reached young Romeo ahead of the Friar's messenger. Rushing to Verona, the disheartened youth paused to purchase a vessel of poison. "Well, Juliet, I will lie with thee tonight," he pledged.

That night Romeo went to Juliet's room; as dawn broke, the lovers could barely let themselves part.

At the Capulet's vaulted tomb, there young Romeo found Paris, also in mourning. Recognizing Romeo, he drew his sword. The two fought and Paris was fatally wounded. In the throes of death, he pled with Romeo to lay him next to his love. Romeo hesitated, then dragged the other man inside the tomb so that he too could lie near Juliet. Then, looking down at his bride, Romeo cried out, "… Eyes, look your last! Arms, take your last embrace! and lips, O you … seal with a righteous kiss a dateless bargain to engrossing death." Leaving a kiss on the beauty's silent lips, Romeo drank the poison and lay motionless by her side.

Soon, Juliet awoke – to find her young husband lying next to her, dead. Hearing footsteps approaching, she unsheathed Romeo's dagger and plunged it into her breast, bewailing, "O happy dagger!… Let me die!"

Just then the Friar entered, followed by the Montagues, the Capulets, and the Prince. Before them lay Paris, along with the limp bodies of the two lovers. At once each family began to cast blame upon the other for the tragedy. The Friar, however, stepped forward and explained the circumstances which had led to the deaths of their tender children, whose only sin was to have loved. When he heard the story, the Prince called out mournfully, "Where be these enemies? Capulet, Montague, see what a scourge is laid upon your hate, that heaven finds means to kill your joys with love.… All are punished."

"O happy dagger!… Let me die!"

At these words, the adversaries clasped hands in brotherhood. "A gloomy peace this morning with it brings," intoned the Prince in a final note, "… for never was a story of more woe than this of Juliet and her Romeo."

COMMENTARY

Perhaps Shakespeare's most famous play, *Romeo and Juliet* combines the contrasting elements of humor and sorrow, bawdiness and civil strife, and innocent love and ignorant hate to rouse an amazing depth of mixed tenderness and tension. Although a Chorus begins the play by notifying the audience that these near-perfect lovers will in the end take their own lives, an irrational sense of hope remains that somehow they might escape their destiny. But the pride-hardened loathing between the feuding families leads the play to its inevitable tragic end.

Moreover, though the drama is one of ultimate reconciliation, ironically, both families lose their only children – neither family line will be carried on. In a sense, Shakespeare is suggesting that war and hate lead, not to victory for either side, but to spiritual annihilation.

Macbeth

TYPE OF WORK

Tragic fatalistic drama

SETTING

Eleventh century Scotland

PRINCIPAL CHARACTERS

Macbeth
A noble Scottish chieftain

Lady Macbeth
His wife

Banquo
Macbeth's warrior-friend

Fleance
Banquo's son

Duncan
King of Scotland, a gentle and perfect ruler

Macduff
A rebel lord

Three Witches

On a stormy night, Scottish armies managed to suppress a rebellion, largely through the valor of two noblemen, Macbeth and Banquo. They also had frustrated a Viking invasion that had received assistance from a prominent Scotsman, the Thane of Cawdor. When news of these two events reached Duncan, King of Scotland, he was delighted with Macbeth's performance, but insisted that Cawdor's treason warranted his death. Accordingly, the king declared that Cawdor be executed and that Macbeth be named in his stead, Thane of Cawdor.

Meanwhile, Macbeth and Banquo, on their way home from war, happened upon a trio of witches – hags stirring a blackened caldron and heralding Macbeth's arrival: "Double, Double, toil and trouble." The witches astonished the pair by prophesying that Macbeth would become first, the new Thane of Cawdor, and then, King of Scotland; and that Banquo would become the father of kings. Then the dark hags vanished, leaving Banquo and Macbeth to speculate over these strange prophecies.

No sooner had the witches departed than two of the king's messengers arrived with news that Macbeth had indeed been named to replace the deposed Thane of Cawdor. Macbeth was amazed to see the first of the witches' prophecies so quickly fulfilled, and began to believe in the ultimate fulfillment of the

"Double, Double, toil and trouble."

second. If he could be Thane of Cawdor, perhaps he could rule all of Scotland as well. This innocent belief quickly expanded into a deep-seated ambition, which began to taint Macbeth's mind with dark thoughts: Would the prophecy fulfill itself, or would he have to take action to usurp the throne? Since Duncan was king, would not one of his two sons follow him in ruling Scotland? All this time, Banquo resisted any thoughts of hastening the witches' prophecy that his children would be kings, but could sense the unrest stirring inside the soul of his fellow officer.

Banquo and Macbeth returned and reported to King Duncan, who warmly commended them both for their courage. But during the ensuing conversation he made two announcements which brought even more sinister ideas into Macbeth's mind: First, the King declared his son, Malcolm, heir to the throne; and second, he expressed his intention to visit Macbeth for a night at Macbeth's castle. Macbeth felt he must somehow take advantage of Duncan's visit to advance his own ambitions – or, as he saw it, his own destiny.

Macbeth was amazed to see the first of the witches' prophecies so quickly fulfilled …

Hearing of her returning husband's success and of the prophecies pronounced upon him, Macbeth's wife was filled with a consuming desire to see him ascend to the throne. Vowing to stop at nothing in this quest, Lady Macbeth urged her husband to help her murder the king as he slept. She would undertake to induce the king's guards to drink, giving Macbeth the opportunity to slip into Duncan's quarters, slay him, and plant the murder weapons on the drunken guards. Macbeth hesitated at first, but his shrewd and aspiring wife eventually prevailed.

As announced, Duncan did visit Macbeth, and after feasting there with Banquo and others, he prepared for bed. According to plan, Lady Macbeth arranged to intoxicate the guards, then sent her husband to do the deed. Presently, Macbeth returned to her, Duncan's murder accomplished. But now Macbeth was brimming with guilt. Nonetheless, the conspiring spouses slipped, unseen, back to their chamber.

Two visiting nobles, Lennox and Macduff, finding the king's lifeless body the next morning, sounded the alarm. Everyone rushed to the site, where Macbeth and his wife pretended to be shocked and heartbroken. Duncan's two sons, suspecting a similar conspiracy would be attempted upon their lives, fled separately to England and Ireland.

After that, events moved swiftly. Everyone saw the flight of Duncan's sons as evidence that they had been the conspirators against their father. Macbeth was crowned as successor to the throne; he had fooled everyone – except Banquo, who was more than a bit suspicious of Macbeth's sudden rise to power.

In fact, Banquo, remembering the promises made by the witches regarding his own progeny, feared jealous attempts on both his life and the life of his son Fleance.

Macbeth felt
he must
somehow take
advantage
of Duncan's
visit to advance
his own
ambitions –
or, as he saw
it, his own
destiny.

Immediately he informed Macbeth that the two of them would be leaving the country.

The tormented new sovereign, who also remembered the witches' ultimate prophecy, hired two assassins to kill Banquo and Fleance as they traveled. He could not allow Banquo's son to rule. Banquo was murdered, but Fleance managed to escape.

Many days later, Macbeth gave a feast for his compatriots. As he raised the glass, mourning that he would have liked his friend Banquo to be present, he was horrified at the appearance of Banquo's bloody ghost – seated on Macbeth's own throne. Now the terrified behavior of their new monarch virtually confirmed to the Scottish nobles that it was Macbeth who had contrived Duncan's assassination. One of the Lords – Macduff – hastily left for England to aid Duncan's avenging son Malcolm in assembling an army to usurp Macbeth.

When Macbeth and his wife learned of this counter plot, they found and consulted the witches for advice. The witches warned them to fear Lord Macduff, but added

Macbeth was crowned as successor to the throne; he had fooled everyone – except Banquo …

that no harm would come to Macbeth "until great Birnham Wood onto high Dunsinane hill shall come." Furthermore, "no man of woman born" should have power to harm him. Macbeth rejoiced: he was assured of ultimate victory. After all, how can a forest move itself? And what man is not born of a woman? But when the witches showed him a vision of eight Kings, Banquo among them, his enthusiasm melted away, and he ordered the prompt slaughter of Macduff's wife and children.

When Macduff, approaching with his armies, learned of these murders, his anguish only sharpened his resolve, and he swore to kill Macbeth with his own sword. When his armies reached Birnham Wood, Macduff instructed each soldier to cut tree boughs and hide behind them, in order to conceal their numbers. Like some kind of walking forest the men moved on Dunsinane, where Macbeth was poised to defend himself.

As Macbeth was preparing for war, his wife, chafing under her own guilty conscience, was walking in her sleep, attempting to wash from her hands invisible bloodstains. The horror of her crimes and the fear of death at the hands of her own untrusting subjects brought on her grim, agonizing dreams. Madness poisoned her spirit so bitterly that, on the eve of Macduff's attack, Lady Macbeth died.

The King's twisted mind too had been nearly destroyed. In his dementia, when word came that his wife had perished, he remained nearly unmoved. Moreover, as he dressed for battle, additional bad news arrived – Birnham Wood seemed to be moving toward them! Macbeth and his army rushed out to meet Macduff's approaching forest of men. Macbeth fought recklessly, only bolstered by the false courage instilled by the witches' pronouncement that "no man born of woman" could overthrow him.

Finally, the two warring leaders engaged in hand-to-hand combat. During the scuffle, Macbeth taunted Macduff; Macduff had not the capacity to kill him:

As easy mayst thou the intrenchant air
With thy keen sword impress as make me bleed.
Let fall thy blade on vulnerable crests.
I bear a charmed life, which must not yield
To one of woman born.

But Macduff, still inflamed over the slaughter of his family, answered his enemy that he had never been, in a sense, "born of woman." "Macduff was from his mother's womb/ Untimely ripped," he replied.

Macbeth now fought in fear, with waning strength. The rebel at last gained the upper hand and plunged his

As he raised the glass … he was horrified at the appearance of Banquo's bloody ghost – seated on Macbeth's own throne.

sword into Macbeth's breast, then severed the head from the body of the bloody counterfeit King of Scotland.

The battle won, Macduff returned to the castle and hailed Malcolm, good King Duncan's rightful heir, the new King of Scotland.

COMMENTARY

This popular, fast-moving and relatively uncomplicated play has become a standard of the effects of ambition. At the outset, Macbeth is perfectly honorable – and the object of special honor from his king. However, the witches' suggestion that he will attain the throne taps the well of ambition in him that (presumably) lies within us all. By the time he has slain Duncan, Macbeth is locked into a career of murder, and eventually becomes so desensitized as to remain unmoved even by his wife's death.

> I bear a charmed life, which must not yield
> To one of woman born.

Granted, Macbeth likely would never have carried out his plans if not spurred on by his wife's stronger personality. In some ways, she is more of a man that he ("Come you spirits," she prays, "unsex me here...."). But in the end she is overcome with guilt that manifests itself in crazed hallucinations.

Only Banquo, among those whose lives were "blessed" by the witches, escapes temptation: first, by refusing the seductions of ambition; and second, by refusing to conspire with Macbeth against Duncan. He is, as the hags rightly prophesy, "lesser than Macbeth, and greater ... not so happy, yet much happier." It is by no accident that Shakespeare's Banquo is a pure, upright fellow. The historical Banquo was the direct ancestor of James I, the King of England at the time of *Macbeth's* first performance.

Othello

TYPE OF WORK

Tragic, romantic drama

SETTING

Venice and the island,
Cyprus; early Sixteenth
century

PRINCIPAL CHARACTERS

Othello
*The Moor of Venice, a black
military man acclaimed for his
conquests*

Desdemona
*His wife, the beautiful daughter
of a government official*

Iago
Othello's devious Ensign

Emilia
*Iago's wife, and attendant
to Desdemona*

Cassio
Othello's devoted Lieutenant

Othello, Moorish commander of the armed forces of
Venice, had secretly married Desdemona, the much
younger daughter of the respected Senator Brabantio.
Capitalizing on this news, Othello's ensign, Iago, who
had earlier professed his desires to Desdemona without
receiving her love in return, sought revenge. Also passed
over for promotion as Othello's new lieutenant chief
of staff, the Moor having chosen instead a loyal
Florentine, Michael Cassio, Iago now devised a scheme
to rid himself of these sorry reminders of his own failings.
He dispatched his inexperienced follower, Roderigo, to
inform Brabantio of the illicit marriage.

The thought of a beguiling Moor marrying his
beloved daughter without consent, led the Senator with
his guards to Othello's house. However, violence was
postponed by the report of an imminent attack on
Cyprus from armed Turkish galleys. The Duke of Venice
summoned Othello to the senate chambers. When
Desdemona appeared and professed her love for Othello,
the Duke cleared him of wrongdoing,
saying to Brabantio, "If virtue no
delighted beauty lack,/ Your son-in-
law is far more fair than black." Then
the Duke directed his courageous
commander to lead the Venetian
forces to Cyprus in its defense.

"If virtue
no delighted
beauty lack,/
Your son-in-law
is far more fair
than black."

With his honor intact, and through Desdemona's pleas to remain with her love, Othello gained permission to have her sail with him. For the voyage, Othello entrusted Desdemona to the care of Iago's wife, Emilia, who did not suspect her husband's treachery. Before the soldier band could reach its enemy, a storm destroyed the Turkish fleet and dispersed the Venetian vessels. Fortunately, all of Othello's ships returned safely to Cyprus and Othello and his bride were reunited.

Iago's hateful plan turned now to lies and innuendo. Seeing the infatuation his pawn Roderigo had for Desdemona, Iago engaged Roderigo in conversation, promising that he could secure for him Desdemona's love:

I hate the Moor. My cause is hearted: thine hath no less reason. Let us be conjunctive in our revenge against him.

The thought of a beguiling Moor's marrying his beloved daughter without consent, led the Senator with his guards to Othello's house.

If thou canst cuckold him, thou dost thyself a pleasure, me a sport.

Iago's hateful plan turned now to lies and innuendo.

But then evil Iago demanded a price for Desdemona: Roderigo would have to engage Cassio in a fight during the lieutenant's night watch. Iago further fanned Roderigo's readiness to kill Cassio by claiming that the Lieutenant was Desdemona's latest love.

That night Iago succeeded in getting Cassio drunk, and the brawl turned to riot. By way of reprimand, Othello was forced to demote Cassio, a severe blow to the high-ranking officer. Desdemona nobly appealed to her husband on Cassio's behalf, in an attempt to revive their friendship. This innocent act provided Iago with yet another idea – a way to convince the Moor of his wife's "natural attraction" to the handsome young Florentine.

Iago approached the despondent Cassio and convinced him that a meeting could be arranged between him and Desdemona; and she could use her influence to have Cassio's position restored. When the meeting took place, Iago drew Othello aside to cause him to see Cassio in the act of "soliciting" his wife. He also began his line of subtle allusions to gossip of a prior romance between the two. His clever suggestions continued, daily planting seeds of jealousy in Othello's heart.

Meanwhile, Desdemona could sense her husband's growing despair. Othello's jealous rages grieved not only her, his ill-starred wife, but also all those under his command. Emilia, Desdemona's loving caretaker, swore of her mistress's fidelity, but the tormented Othello would not listen.

Iago's plan was promoted even more when he obtained a handkerchief Othello had given to Desdemona as a love token. It had been found by Emilia, who intended to return it to her mistress. Instead, Iago secretly planted it in Cassio's bed.

Tortured over the weeks, and weary of Iago's incessant insinuations, Othello finally demanded proof from his Ensign of Desdemona's unfaithfulness:

> *Villain, be sure thou prove my love a whore,*
> *Or by the worth of man's eternal soul,*
> *Thou hadst been better have been born a dog*
> *Than answer my wak'd wrath....*

Iago swore to have heard Cassio speak words of love to Desdemona in his sleep. As additional evidence he cited having seen Cassio wipe his beard with the missing scarf, which Cassio had since discovered in his quarters. Iago's cunning scheme was working; Othello was finally convinced:

> Othello: *Get me some poison, Iago, this night....*
> Iago: *Do it not with poison. Strangle her in her bed, even the bed she hath contaminated.*
> Othello: *Good, good. The justice of it pleases. Very good.*
> Iago: *And for Cassio, let me be his undertaker....*

Overwhelmed with madness, Othello at once accepted Iago's words, making him his new lieutenant and charging him with his first order of business: Kill the deceitful Cassio.

In treacherous obedience to this commander, Iago enlisted Roderigo to ambush Cassio. With Iago hiding in the night's darkness, Roderigo confronted Cassio in a duel,

Iago drew Othello aside to cause him to see Cassio in the act of "soliciting" his wife.

but was wounded himself. Then, in the scuffle, Iago leaped out and wounded Cassio. In order to keep Roderigo from talking, Iago next turned on Roderigo, fatally stabbing the unfortunate lackey.

A crowd quickly gathered, including a harlot who claimed wounded Cassio as a friend. Iago, reasoning that a broken and a shunned Cassio would be an even sweeter revenge than a dead Cassio, decided this woman could be used to further defame his enemy. Pretending to have been a passer-by coming to Cassio's aid, Iago, along with some other Venetian gentlemen, assisted the wounded lieutenant toward Othello's home.

That same evening, Othello ordered Desdemona to excuse her servant early and retire to bed. In an anguished fit of passion, he then entered her chamber and kissed her:

Emilia, Desdemona's loving caretaker, swore of her mistress' fidelity, but the tormented Othello would not listen.

Othello: *Have you pray'd tonight, Desdemon?*
Desdemona: *Ay, my lord.*
Othello: *If you bethink yourself of any crime*
unreconcil'd as yet to heaven and grace,
solicit for it straight....
I would not kill thy unprepared spirit ...

Othello then spelled out the evidence which accused her of her crime, and demanded a confession. Desdemona denied any impropriety; Cassio must have found the handkerchief.... But Othello spoke up, reporting that Cassio, her very lover, had already been justly assassinated. Desdemona burst into tears. "O strumpet! Weep'st thou for him in my face?" the husband cried. And then, despite her pleadings, he smothered her with a pillow.

The act completed, Othello was interrupted by Emilia at the door. She entered and told the Moor that Roderigo had been killed, but Cassio yet lived. Distraught, and seeking to justify his wife's murder, Othello disclosed to Emilia how he knew of his dead wife's infidelity – "... Thy husband knew it all.... My friend, thy husband, honest, honest Iago," he had made the accusation.

When Iago, Cassio and the nobles arrived, Emilia urged her husband to refute Othello's claim. Upon seeing the falseness reflected in Iago's eyes, however, and beholding his vain attempts to absolve himself, the general suddenly realized the tragic error he had made. His trusted Ensign had orchestrated the entire affair. The missing scarf, the meeting between Cassio and Desdemona, the cause of his insane grief – all was Iago's doing.

Emilia became sickened at the reality of her husband's villainy. Amid sobs of grief, she began

> Do it not with poison. Strangle her in her bed, even the bed she hath contaminated.

If you be think yourself of any crime ...

Unreconcil'd as yet to heaven and grace, Solicit for it traight....

I would not kill thy unprepared spirit ...

to rebuke him. Impulsively, Iago drew his dagger and stabbed his frenzied wife. Othello lunged at Iago, wounding him, but was restrained by the nobles from finishing the deed.

Faithful Emilia died, still calmly defending Desdemona's innocence and proclaiming her love for the virtuous woman. Othello, on the other hand, mad with guilt and sorrow, pleaded with his true friend, Cassio:

> ... *When you shall these unlucky deeds relate,*
> *Speak of them as they are. Nothing extenuate,*
> *Nor set down in malice. Then must you speak*
> *Of one that lov'd not wisely but too well;*
> *Of one not easily jealous, but, being wrought,*
> *Perplex'd in the extreme; of one whose hand*
> *... threw a pearl away....*

The missing scarf, the meeting between Cassio and Desdemona, the cause of his insane grief – all was Iago's doing.

This said, Othello raised his dagger and thrust its blade into his own heart. As he lay dying, he could only be content with the promise that wicked, traitorous Iago would be tortured to death at the hands of the governor-general of Cyprus.

COMMENTARY

Shakespeare's *Othello* epitomizes the playwright's masterful ability to weave his characters' intricate motives and acts into one smooth plot. Of all his villains, Iago seems to be the most complete and sadistic, with no greater motive than wounded pride for his wickedness. Indeed, the drama might well be named "Iago," since he is the character most prominent throughout.

But the character most discussed by critics continues to be Othello. Is he an honorable, tragic hero who is ennobled by the unsuspecting confidence he places in his advisor? Or is he nothing more than a vulnerable, murderous and tragic fool? Othello himself recognizes this extraordinary paradox when, at the end of the play, he describes himself as "an honourable murderer"; as "one that loved not wisely but too well."

In contrast, we experience the authentic bond of love between two faithful women. And ultimately, love triumphs – even if only in death – over pride, envy, hate and evil.

Julius Caesar

TYPE OF WORK

Tragic drama

SETTING

Rome; 44 B.C.E.

PRINCIPAL CHARACTERS

Julius Caesar
Popular Roman general and statesman

Brutus
A prominent and devout Roman, and close friend to Caesar

Cassius
A conspiring enemy of Caesar

Marcus Antonius
Caesar's supporter, a brilliant politician

Rome was in an uproar. General Julius Caesar had just
returned after having defeated his rival, Pompey.
His many military triumphs had made him the most
powerful man in Rome. The commoners – blindly
cheering whomever was in power – flocked into the
streets to hail him.

A s Caesar passed through the city, a soothsayer
caught his attention and called out: "Beware the Ides
of March." But the general ignored the warning; he was too
busy refusing the crown offered to him by his compatriot
and fellow politician, Marcus Antonius. This humble
denial of power fanned within the masses an even greater
devotion to their beloved Caesar.

Meanwhile, among the throng stood Cassius,
Caesar's avowed political opponent, and Brutus, the
general's personal friend. Envious of Caesar's growing
popularity, Cassius probed to discover where
Brutus's deepest sympathies lay. He voiced a concern
he had: Caesar was becoming overly "ambitious." Unless
something was done to check his fame, he would soon
seize all power for himself. This could, effectively, turn
the Roman Republic into a dictatorship. Cassius then
apprised Brutus of a plot he had hatched: He and a band
of other prominent Romans were planning to
assassinate Caesar. Was Brutus willing to join in the
conspiracy?

Brutus admitted that he shared the same inner concern: "I do fear the people choose Caesar for their king." But still Brutus hesitated to involve himself in such a plot. After all, he dearly loved and admired Caesar. Even so, he couldn't deny that Caesar's rapid rise to power constituted a potential threat to the Republic. Brutus promised Cassius that he would consider the matter, but would withhold his decision until the following day.

Should he aid in the killing of his beloved friend Caesar, or should he sit by and watch as Caesar destroyed the State?

The dilemma weighed upon Brutus throughout the night: should he aid in the killing of his beloved friend Caesar, or should he sit by and watch as Caesar destroyed the State?

The plotting band, hoping to gain the support of the highly respected Brutus, paid him an early morning visit. Referring to Caesar as an "immortal god," presenting false evidence of his intentions, and playing on Brutus's immense love for Rome, Cassius finally prevailed on him to help see to the man's death. Brutus reluctantly agreed to take part in his friend's assassination, to "think of him as a serpent's egg, which, hatched, would as his kind, grow mischievous, and kill him in the shell." Assassination – a certain "righteous treason" – Brutus decided, was justified under the circumstances.

Caesar had announced that he would appear before a vast crowd at the Capitol the next morning – the Ides of March. There the conspirators planned to attack and dagger him to death.

After an eerie night, filled with reports of gaping graves and wandering ghosts throughout the city, Caesar set out early toward the Capitol, despite three separate warnings: an oracle, the self same soothsayer from before, and finally, his wife, Calpurnia, who experienced a violent and horrible dream, all prophesied that his life was in jeopardy.

As predicted, while Caesar stood addressing the multitude, his conspirators surrounded him and stabbed him, one by one. As Brutus finally stepped forward to thrust his dagger into his friend's side, Caesar whispered, "Et tu, Brute?" ("You too, Brutus?"). The great general then fell dead from twenty-three knife wounds.

The onlooking Romans were stunned and horrified, and Brutus immediately arranged for a public funeral where he could placate the masses by justifying the killing. Then the conspirators bathed their hands in Caesar's blood and marched through the marketplace, brandishing their weapons over their heads, crying, "Peace, freedom, and liberty!"

At the funeral, Brutus sought to convince the angry mourners why it was requisite that Caesar die. Despite his love for Caesar, Brutus frankly and honestly felt that he had been forced to kill his general in order to save Rome

Assassination – a certain "righteous treason" – Brutus reluctantly decided, was justified under the circumstances.

As Brutus finally stepped forward to thrust his dagger into his friend's side, Caesar whispered, "Et tu, Brute?"

from dictatorship. "Not that I loved Caesar less, but that I loved Rome more," he began.

"Not that I loved Caesar less, but that I loved Rome more ..."

As Caesar loved me, I weep for him; as he was fortunate, I rejoice at it; as he was valiant, I honour him; but, as he was ambitious, I slew him. There are tears, for his love; joy, for his fortune; honour, for his valor; and death for his ambition.... As I slew my best lover for the good of Rome, I have the same dagger for myself when it shall please my country to need my death.

His eloquence won over the heart of every Roman in the throng. They forgave Brutus and even cried, "Let him be Caesar!" But then, ill-advisedly, Brutus invited Marcus Antonius, Caesar's right-hand man, to address the crowd. Though Antonius had pretended at the time to tolerate the conspirators and accept their action, in fact, he regarded them as "butchers," and secretly vowed to avenge the murder. Antonius rose to deliver an even more brilliant and impassioned speech, in which he defended Caesar and forcefully, yet indirectly, condemned Brutus:

Friends, Romans, countrymen, lend me your ears; I come to bury Caesar, not to praise him. The evil that men do lives after them, the good is oft interred with their bones; so let it be with Caesar.

The noble Brutus hath told you Caesar was ambitious; If it were so, it was a grievous fault, and grievously hath Caesar answer'd it, here, under leave of Brutus and the rest.... For Brutus is an honourable man; so are they all, all honourable men.

Come I to speak in Caesar's funeral. He was my friend, faithful and just to me: But Brutus says he was ambitious: And Brutus is an honourable man. He [Caesar] hath brought many captives home to Rome, whose ransoms did the general coffers fill; Did this in Caesar seem ambitious? When that the poor have cried, Caesar hath wept; ambition should be made of sterner stuff: Yet Brutus says he was ambitious; And Brutus is an honourable man. You all did see that on the Lupercal I thrice presented him a kingly crown, which he did thrice refuse: was this ambition? Yet Brutus says he was ambitious; And, surely, he is an honourable man....

Friends, Romans, countrymen, lend me your ears; I come to bury Caesar, not to praise him.

Antonius's listeners were so moved by his words that they now turned in rage against Brutus, driving him and his cohorts from the city. Then Antonius, with the help and encouragement of his friend, Octavian, an adopted relative of Caesar's, raised an army to hunt down the confederates.

But Brutus, having fled to Sardis, mustered his own army to counter this attack. Joined by Cassius and other insurgents, he determined to meet Antonius's troops at Phillipi.

The night before the battle, however, everything went askew for Brutus and his allies. Cassius and Brutus quarreled constantly over military strategy; then news came that Brutus's wife, ashamed by her husband's actions, had killed herself at Rome; and, if this were not enough, Brutus received a visit to his tent from an alarming guest: none other than the Ghost of Caesar himself. The tide of fortune had long turned against the conspirators; they were soundly defeated the next day. In the heat of battle, Cassius, rather than be captured, took his life with his own sword, while calling up slain Caesar's otherworldly spirit with the words: "Caesar, thou art revenged, even with the sword that killed thee." Brutus, spotting Cassius's body, likewise sensed the presence of Caesar's ghost, and cried, "O Julius Caesar, thou art mighty yet!"

When Brutus found his army surrounded, he begged that his men kill him. They refused. The commander then ordered a servant to hold his sword and to avert his face, whereupon Brutus ran onto the sword and died an agonizing death.

Before returning to Rome, Octavian, the future emperor, along with Caesar's loyal friend Antonius, paid tribute to Brutus; for here was a man, struggling in the midst of a tragic clash between two great loyalties, who, though deceived, had proved with his own blood and the blood of a friend he loved, his unconquerable devotion to his country. "This was the noblest Roman of them all...."

COMMENTARY

The reader cannot study *Julius Caesar* with an eye to learning Roman history. As usual, Shakespeare

When that the poor have cried, Caesar hath wept; ambition should be made of sterner stuff ...

significantly alters actual sequences and events.
For instance, the play is compressed into six days' time,
while the events, as recorded in history, took place over the
space of three years.

The play's central figure turns out to be not Julius
Caesar at all, but Brutus, who (like Hamlet) feels
compelled to commit a murder for the sake of a principle.
All his life noble Brutus had been faithful; and through
a labyrinthine tangle of plots, politics and power bids,
he had distinguished himself for his integrity, honor and
courage, so that, even after his defeat, his enemies
recognize him as their moral superior.

Aside from the political intrigue of the plot, the play
is filled with brilliant speeches, timeless both for their
declamatory techniques and for the passions they reflect
and evoke. Read from Cassius's speech as he fumes over
Caesar's faults; or turn to the touching plea of Brutus's wife
for her husband to surrender and return home to her.
And certainly, the two speeches delivered by Brutus and
Antonius at the funeral are classics in oratory.

"Caesar, thou art revenged, even with the sword that killed thee."

Shakespeare at a Glance

Comedies

Tragedies

Histories

"I do believe … that you are mine enemy; [but] you shall not be my judge."

Henry VIII

Was he a "king"? Or was he a "beggar"?
Or was he simply "nothing" at all?
At last he concluded, "I waste time, and
now doth Time waste me."

Richard II

"O fair Katharine, if you will love me
soundly with your French heart, I will be
glad to hear you confess it brokenly with
your English tongue."

Henry V

"A horse! My kingdom for a horse!"

Richard III

"Things won are done," she mused. Men prize the thing ungained...." Troilus and Cressida

Troilus and Cressida

Where Antony preferred an untamed, garrulous woman, Octavia was a woman of most "holy, cold, and still conversation."

Antony and Cleopatra

Antony and Cleopatra

TYPE OF WORK

Passionate tragedy

SETTING

Alexandria, Egypt
and Rome, Italy
c. 40–30 B.C.E.

PRINCIPAL CHARACTERS

Antony
A leader of the Roman triumvirate

Cleopatra
*A beautiful and clever Egyptian
Queen*

Caesar and Lepidus
*Other Roman leaders of the
triumvirate*

Pompey
A powerful Roman rebel

Octavia
*Caesar's sister and Antony's
second wife*

Enobarbus
Antony's wise friend and counselor

Antony first met Cleopatra when she was the mistress of Julius Caesar. Their affair began when Cleopatra, draped in gold and highly perfumed, sailed on a barge down the river Cydrus to meet Antony on matters of state. His passion for her intensified as the years passed – and frequently kept him from his duties in Rome. While Antony luxuriated in Alexandria with Cleopatra, Lepidus and Caesar, the other two members of the Roman triumvirate jointly leading the Roman Empire, struggled with the threat of the insurrectionist Pompey, who continually pirated Roman fleets.

Attended by their friends and servants, Antony and Cleopatra enjoyed every sensual pleasure in the palace at Alexandria. Antony's friends, however, were troubled by his cravings for the Egyptian Queen. One of them complained that Antony's doting surpassed "the measure" of good sense and that the mighty Roman leader had been reduced to "a strumpet's fool." But such thoughts certainly did not worry Cleopatra – who reveled in her lover's attentions – although she did have a concern of her own, namely, Antony's wife, Fulvia.

Finally, when jealousy overcame her, Cleopatra sought proof of Antony's love for her. One day when a messenger from Rome arrived, Cleopatra noticed the frown on Antony's face, an expression she attributed to a mysterious "Roman thought." After leaving him with the messenger, she commanded one of her attendants to summon Antony to her side. Then, the moment he arrived, she feigned illness, hoping that he would dote on her. Antony did not oblige. Suspecting it was Fulvia who preoccupied his mind, Cleopatra bristled with resentment, saying, "Hers you are."

Perhaps amused by her passionate outburst, Antony listened intently to his lover's tirade. Then he interrupted, informing her that he had to return to Rome, now besieged by Pompey's ships. This said, he stunned Cleopatra with more interesting news: Fulvia was dead. Cleopatra's reaction to these tidings greatly surprised Antony; she explained haughtily that surely her own death would someday be "received" as Fulvia's had been – coldly. After comforting her, he then took his leave, assuring that his heart would "remain" with her.

When Antony arrived in Rome, he met with his fellow magistrates Lepidus and Caesar. Caesar had most strongly disapproved of Antony's sojourn in Alexandria, complaining to Lepidus that the general not only was in neglect of his stately duties, but "he fishes, drinks, and wastes" his time. But now, confronted with the threat of

Perhaps amused by her passionate outburst, Antony listened intently to his lover's tirade.

Pompey's forces, Caesar ceased his murmuring; saving Rome was paramount, and they would have to consolidate their forces in order to win. Upon greeting Antony anew, however, he was unable to resist a brief chastisement, reminding Antony that he had reacted to his letters "with taunts" and that Fulvia and Antony's brother had conspired to overthrow Caesar. Antony insisted that he had no part in his family's conspiracies. Lepidus mediated, and Antony and Caesar reconciled their immediate differences.

Finally, when jealousy overcame her, Cleopatra sought proof of Antony's love for her.

In fact, at the suggestion of one of Caesar's friends, the two cemented their alliance through marriage: Antony agreed to wed Caesar's sister, Octavia, after professing that he had become wise from past mistakes and that thereafter, in his devotion to Octavia, all would be "done by th' rule."

Antony's friend and faithful counselor Enobarbus, though, rightfully doubted Antony's devotion to Octavia. As he conjured up in his mind Cleopatra's figure adorned in "cloth-of-gold-of-tissue" riding upon her gold-leafed barge, Enobarbus knew that Antony would never forsake the allure of the beautiful Egyptian Queen.

Back in Egypt, when Cleopatra received news of Antony's marriage, she became heartbroken and, characteristically, enraged. She first threatened to stab the messenger, then quickly reconsidered; she could make good use of the man. He would return to Rome and bring back to her a description of her new rival's "years," "her inclination," and "the color of her hair." Indeed, Cleopatra already sensed that Octavia presented little threat to her: where Antony preferred an untamed, garrulous woman,

Octavia was a woman of most "holy, cold, and still conversation."

Elsewhere, Pompey, Rome's nemesis, also recognized that Octavia could not hold Antony. Summoned to Rome to effect a truce, the enemy general speculated that, "first or last," Cleopatra's charms would again win Antony.

Before long, Pompey's words proved true. On a state visit to Athens, Antony declared a separation from Octavia after learning that, in his absence, her brother, Caesar, had broken the truce with Pompey. Subsequently, Caesar had stripped Lepidus of his power and sentenced him to death. Vowing to "raise the preparation of a war on Caesar," Antony immediately sent Octavia back to Rome, while once more he set sail for Alexandria.

In her palace, Cleopatra had been greatly relieved to hear her messenger's depiction of Octavia: her lover's wife was rather "dull of tongue and dwarfish." Again confident of Antony's devotions, on his return to Alexandria she

… when Cleopatra received news of Antony's marriage, she became heart-broken and, characteristically, enraged.

used her wiles to persuade him to extend her sovereignty beyond Egypt, united her forces with his in a war against Caesar, and insisted on being with Antony on the battlefield. Only Enobarbus dared caution that her presence would take Antony's "heart," "brain," and "time" away from matters of war. But Cleopatra would not listen. Instead, she urged Antony to assemble his forces together with her own fleet to meet Caesar's troops at sea. Enobarbus candidly tried to dissuade Antony from waging a sea battle, for the army was trained for land warfare, but Antony dismissed his friend's advice.

In time, Antony and Cleopatra's forces clashed with Caesar's ships. In the midst of battle at Actium, however, Cleopatra abruptly changed her mind and commanded her ships to return to Alexandria. Antony panicked, "leaving the fight in height," and followed Cleopatra. Back in the palace, Antony brooded, dejected. The earth was "ashamed to bear" him, he concluded; he had "lost command." Even Cleopatra could not soften his sorrow. When she came to him, he wailed, "O, whither hast thou led me, Egypt?" She beseeched her lover's pardon, and he forgave her, saying, "Fall not a tear"; to him, each one of her tears was worth "all that is won and lost."

Soon, however, they comprehended the enormity of their defeat. Caesar, gloating in his victory, sent word to Cleopatra that, in exchange for the "grizzled head" of Antony, he would give her whatever she wished. Outraged, Antony challenged Caesar to meet him "sword against sword"; Caesar, of course, declined to duel. By now desperate for some sort of victory, Antony wondered: Why not lead another army against Caesar? Elated by this new plan, he and Cleopatra celebrated – to feast and "mock the midnight bell."

When Antony awoke the next morning, his thoughts were already on battle, and he immediately began to don his armor. When Cleopatra tried to help him, Antony told her happily that she was the "armorer" of his heart. Then he kissed her and set out for his camp. There he heard troubling news: trusted Enobarbus had defected over to Caesar's camp. Within days, however, overcome with remorse for having deserted his friend, the man set off to find "some ditch wherein to die."

Caesar, gloating in his victory, sent word that, in exchange for the "grizzled head" of Antony, he would give Cleopatra whatever she wished.

Antony never did learn of Enobarbus's death. Busy with the intricacies of warfare, he had another reason to despair. From his vantage point in Alexandria, he watched as the Egyptian fleets again turned and fled from the fight. "All is lost," he grieved. Then, convinced that Cleopatra was to blame, he raged, "The foul Egyptian hath betrayed me…. Fortune and Antony part here."

Upon hearing that Antony considered her both a false lover and a false fellow ally, Cleopatra, greatly saddened, longed once more to have him at her side. In a clever ploy to bring him there, she dispatched an attendant to inform her love that she had died and that her body had been taken to her monument.

"All length is torture; since the torch is out," Antony cried out upon hearing the news. Then, turning to one of his men, he commanded him to kill him with his sword. The reluctant soldier finally did lift his sword and said, "Farewell, great chief." Antony bravely awaited the act, but was stunned when the man instead plunged the sword into his own breast, in order to "escape the sorrow" of witnessing his commander's death.

"Thou teachest me," Antony lamented. Then he fell on his own sword – but, alas, he did not die. "O dispatch me!" he called out. When Antony's men came running to his side, he pled with them to put him to death. But no one dared.

Soon, another of Cleopatra's attendants arrived, breathlessly explaining that news of the Egyptian's death had been a ploy. Mortally wounded, Antony groaned, "Bear me, good friends, where Cleopatra bides." The Roman soldiers quickly conveyed Antony to Cleopatra's monument, constructed to serve as her tomb. Embracing and kissing him, Cleopatra condemned her foolish actions. Antony, however, forgave her. Then, before waning into death, sought to comfort his beloved:

In a clever ploy to bring him there, she dispatched an attendant to tell Antony that she had died and that her body had been taken to her monument.

The miserable change now at my end
Lament nor sorrow at; but please your thoughts
In feeding them with those my former fortunes
Wherein I liv'd, the greatest prince o' th' world....

Cleopatra, overcome with anguish, resolved soon to
join him.

In Rome, meanwhile, Caesar, learning of Antony's
death, did not rejoice; rather, he mourned him as a
"brother" and as a "mate in empire." Then he dispatched
a messenger to invite Cleopatra to Rome, where he would
treat her most "humble and kindly." Others had already
unmasked Caesar's true intentions: she knew that he
would make her his captive, parade her through the streets,
and let her be "chastised by the sober eye" of her rival
Octavia. Nevertheless, Cleopatra accepted the invitation.

Before Caesar and his men arrived to convey her to
Rome, however, Cleopatra arranged for a peasant to bring
her a basket of figs. "Hast thou the pretty worm of Nilus
there, that kills and pains not?" Cleopatra asked the man.
He assured her he did. Indeed, among the figs deadly asps

Mortally wounded, Antony said, "Bear me, good friends where Cleopatra bides."

slithered in the basket. Once Cleopatra had dismissed the man, she asked one of her attendants to dress her in her robe and crown. Putting an asp to her breast, Cleopatra then bade the serpent, "Be angry, and dispatch," and, before dying, called out, "O Antony!"

When Caesar and his men entered the monument, they found the bodies of the Egyptian Queen and two of her attendants. "She shall be buried by her Antony," Caesar declared as he marveled at the "pity" and the "glory" of the amorous and tempestuous couple.

COMMENTARY

*A*ntony and Cleopatra depicts a world rife with opposing forces: honor clashing with dishonor, fidelity with promiscuity, domination with subjugation, trust with treachery. Overriding the character flaws, however, is one primary conflict between all that is "Roman" and all that is "Egyptian." "While there is one world in the play," critic Northrop Frye points out, "there are two aspects of it: the aspect of 'law and order' represented by Rome and the aspect of sexual extravagance and license represented by Egypt."

Shakespeare uses a particularly clearheaded character, Enobarbus, to illuminate this conflict. A somewhat insignificant player in the drama, Enobarbus is free to speculate on the relative attributes of both nation-states. His primary role is to highlight the contrast between the intoxicating sensuality of Cleopatra's Egypt and the established mores of Antony's Rome – which Antony ultimately betrays to passion.

Troilus and Cressida

It was the seventh year of the Trojan War. Helen, whose abduction from her husband Menelaus had caused the Greeks to lay siege to Troy, remained with her Trojan abductor Paris behind the city's walls. For the first time since the war began, Greeks and Trojans alike were questioning their motives and their resolve to fight.

The Greek army had fallen into chaos. Although in numbers they were superior to the Trojans, their morale had so deteriorated that any possibility of victory now appeared to be extremely remote. As Ulysses, one of the Greek commanders, noted to King Agamemnon, they lacked unity and order. It was their own disarray that was defeating them: "Troy in our weakness stands, not in her strength."

Agamemnon quizzed the General as to how the Greeks might remedy the situation, and Ulysses replied quite simply: "Achilles" – the Greeks' champion warrior. The one impediment?: Achilles refused to fight. He was in love with the Trojan Princess Polyxena, and Polyxena's mother, Queen Hecuba, had made her daughter's suitor promise that he would not take part in the siege. By some means, Ulysses concluded,

> Achilles was the Greeks' champion warrior. The problem was, however, that he refused to fight.

Achilles and his Myrmidon soldiers must be humbled and roused to come to Greece's aid.

The Trojans, on the other hand, had begun to wonder aloud whether Helen merited their years of suffering. The Greeks had once more sent an emissary to Troy, asking its King Priam to deliver Helen over to them and thus end the war. Priam was now seriously considering this possibility; even his eldest son, Prince Hector, was forced to admit that his sister-in-law Helen was "not worth what she doth cost – the keeping."

The young, idealistic Trojan Prince Troilus, however, vehemently disagreed; Helen, now the captive wife of his brother, Paris, could not "honorably" be surrendered. After all, Paris, against heavy odds, had managed to ensnare her and bring her back to Troy. But Troilus, as he argued with his father and brother against returning Helen to the Greeks, was perhaps motivated by his own fortunes in love, for he had fallen for the beautiful Cressida, a Trojan native. But in spite of the fact that Cressida was within arm's reach, Troilus had been unable to win her affections. Indeed, Cressida appeared to be wholly unaware of his existence.

Against this uncertain backdrop – the fortunes of love entangled with those of war – Cressida's uncle, the diseased

… once a wife was taken she could not "honorably" be surrendered …

and decrepit Pandarus, pleaded with Troilus not to lose hope. Troilus by now had grown impatient with Pandarus's attempts to bring him and Cressida together, and Pandarus took offense at this attitude, complaining of "small thanks for my labor."

"[Have] you any eyes?" Pandarus asked Cressida, "Do you know what a man is?

Nevertheless, he persisted, taking every opportunity to promote Troilus's interests with his niece. "[Have] you any eyes?" Pandarus asked Cressida. "Do you know what a man is? Is not birth, beauty, good shape, discourse, manhood, learning, gentleness, virtue, youth, liberality, and such like, the spice and salt that season a man?"

Cressida, for her part, pretended to be unmoved by her uncle's appeals – although, in fact, she held Troilus in some regard. She considered this feigned lack of interest to be a necessary tactic in love. A man's passions and desires could be more fully aroused, she had discovered, when she pretended to withhold her own. "Things won are done," she mused. "Men prize the thing ungained...."

This strategy, however, was neither unique to Cressida nor confined merely to games of love; variations of it were also applied to games of war. The Greeks' petition for Helen's release had been answered by a summons from Hector that each army's best soldier meet in single combat – a development that led back to the Greeks' quandary with Achilles, since Hector's challenge had clearly been intended for this heroic son of a goddess and a king. After some debate, however, it was decided that Ajax – not Achilles – should meet Hector. "Ajax employed," reasoned Ulysses, "plucks down Achilles' plumes."

In Troy, meanwhile, Pandarus had at last succeeded in persuading Cressida to meet with Troilus. Troilus was

A man's passions and desires could be more fully aroused, she had discovered, when she pretended to withhold her own.

ecstatic. "Expectation," he told Pandarus, "whirls me round. Th' imaginary relish is so sweet/That it enchants my sense." The night's tryst disappointed neither of the lovers. When morning finally broke, Cressida turned to Troilus and ruefully complained, "Night hath been too brief." The liaison was briefer, though, than even she could have imagined, for that very night Cressida's father – who years earlier had defected to the Greeks – had authored an agreement by which Cressida would be exchanged for a Trojan prisoner of war. This agreement of exchange was a fait accompli: the Greek commander Diomedes appeared at that moment to escort her to her father's tent. The distraught pair pledged their mutual love, and, as a token of enduring faithfulness, Troilus gave Cressida his sleeve and promised her that somehow, no matter what the dangers to him, he would visit her every night in the Greek encampment. Then Cressida was led off to her father.

… there was nothing Achilles could do but watch as the enemy armies assembled outside Troy for the match between their respective champions.

By now, Achilles had heard of Hector's challenge – and that Agamemnon had selected Ajax for the match. He took this news as an insult; Ajax was a fool. "What, are [my] deeds forgot?" he asked Ulysses. Inwardly, Ulysses smiled. His strategy with Achilles – like Cressida's with Troilus – seemed to be working. His reply now pressed the ploy carefully home:

Those scraps are good deeds past,
Which are devour'd as fast as they are made,
Forgot as soon as done. Perseverance, dear my lord,

Keeps honor bright. To have done, is to hang
Quite out of fashion....

Much as he loathed it, that evening there was nothing Achilles could do but watch as the enemy armies assembled outside Troy for the match between their respective champions. Hector, who had hoped to meet Achilles on the field, was greatly dismayed to find Ajax in his place: he had not expected that the Greeks would choose his own cousin as his foe. After parrying a few sword thrusts, he honorably declined to continue the match against the son of his mother's sister. The Greeks and Trojans, it was decided, would enjoy a brief respite and feast each other that night. Tomorrow the war would resume.

The Greeks and Trojans would enjoy a brief respite and feast each other that night. Tomorrow the war would resume.

That night, Achilles invited Hector to his tent. He had finally given in to the calls to fight, and, as he told his friend Patroclus, this would be an opportunity to size up his foe. "I'll heat his blood with Greekish wine tonight," he hissed, "which with my scimitar I'll cool tomorrow."

Troilus also found in this unforeseen turn of events a wonderful opportunity: now he could see Cressida. But as he approached the tent of his beloved, he heard voices from within. It was Cressida and Diomedes, who, earlier that same morning, had introduced himself as her escort from Troy. Yet here he was in her tent, and here she was trying to persuade him not to leave, calling after him, in a plaintive voice, "Sweet honey Greek."

Cressida and Diomedes were having what appeared to be a lovers' quarrel – and the quarrel appeared to revolve around the sleeve Troilus had given her that morning as a pledge and token of his love. Cressida had obviously given the sleeve to Diomedes but, having reconsidered, wanted it back. Diomedes refused, and was now demanding to know whose sleeve it was. "Tomorrow," Diomedes said, "I'll wear it on my helmet, and grieve his spirit that dares not challenge it."

Troilus was stunned by these words, utterly crushed by Cressida's fickle, duplicitous nature. This both was and was not his Cressida, he thought. Turning to Ulysses, he swore that the following day, when the Trojans again met the Greeks on the battlefield, he would have his revenge on Diomedes:

> As much as I do Cressid love,
> So much by weight hate I her Diomed.
> That sleeve is mine that he'll bear on his helmet;
> Were it a casque compos'd by Vulcan's skill,
> My sword should bite it.…

As the next day's campaign wore to its close, the fighting – typical of the last several years' battles – yielded neither side the advantage. Troilus had found and fought Diomedes on the field, but, apart from Troilus's losing his horse, nothing conclusive had come of their confrontation.

Hector, who had been victorious all day, was preparing to retire from the field. He had just disarmed himself and turned toward Troy when Achilles reappeared. The two had met in combat earlier that day, but after parrying only a short time, Achilles had asked Hector's permission to withdraw, claiming that he was too tired to fight on. Now, however,

"I'll heat his blood with Greekish wine tonight," he said, "which with my scimitar I'll cool tomorrow."

presented with such an easy target, Achilles ordered his Myrmidon spearmen to kill Hector. He then tied the dead corpse to the tail of his horse and, in full view of the returning Trojans, dragged the dishonored Trojan general's body through the fields.

All of Troy was grief-stricken. All swore vengeance on the Greeks for the cowardly and treacherous act Achilles had committed. Troilus passed slowly through the gates of Troy, and, as he entered the city, heard the sickly, disease-ridden Pandarus call out to him, "But hear you, hear you!" He looked up and called back to Pandarus, "Hence, broker, lackey! Ignominy and shame pursue thy life, and live aye thy name."

COMMENTARY

One of Shakespeare's most elusive works, *Troilus and Cressida* occupies a peculiar place in the Shakespearian canon: variously classified as a history, a comedy, and a tragedy, the play turns on an unusual, highly contrapuntal – and strangely frustrating – double plot. The first concerns the Trojan War and revolves primarily around the characters of Hector and Achilles; the second is the love story involving Troilus and Cressida. What makes this double plot both intriguing and, finally, unsatisfying, is that both sides of the story have what A.P. Rossiter calls a "false bottom"; that is, each plot line builds dramatic tension and rises to a climax, creating expectations which the play's action then refuses to fulfill.

Turning to Ulysses, he swore that the next day, when the Trojans again met the Greeks on the battlefield, he would have his revenge on Diomedes …

The tension, for instance, that builds around the long-anticipated combat scenes between the opposing champions Hector and Achilles is deflated not once, but twice. Similarly, the love story between Troilus and Cressida turns out to climax not in resolution, but instead in duplicity, deception and disillusionment. Even the dramatic tension that builds after Troilus and Diomedes pledge to take revenge on each other is deflated, neither fulfilling his pledge.

... presented with such an easy target, Achilles ordered his Myrmidon spearmen to kill Hector.

By the play's end, the Greeks have finally obtained an apparent advantage over Troy. It is, however, an ill-gotten advantage. Contrary to the tradition of the Homeric epic, Hector's death is achieved not through heroic combat but through a cowardly act of murder.

Troilus and Cressida is nevertheless a brilliant play, characterized by its biting and caustic wit. Still, there are no heroes in this tragedy. Indeed, Shakespeare, perhaps anticipating the existentialist pessimism of the 20th century in this Elizabethan drama, gives the last word to the sickly Pandarus, who turns to address the audience, first to bewail his own misfortunes, and second, in an unnerving gesture, "to bequeath you my diseases."

The Life of King Henry V

TYPE OF WORK

Patriotic war drama

SETTING

England and France;
c. 1415

PRINCIPAL CHARACTERS

Henry V
King of England

Archbishop of Canterbury
The King's advisor

Charles VI
King of France

Princess Katharine
Charles's daughter

The Dauphin
Charles's son, the Crown Prince

Pistol
A poor Englishman who goes to war

Boy
*An English child who accompanies
Pistol*

Mountjoy
A French messenger

In Shakespeare's two plays that make up Henry IV, a young Henry V underwent a profound metamorphosis. He had grown from a rakish prince who passed many idle hours at the Boar's Head Tavern into a shrewd young man. And as Henry V listened carefully to the advice of his dying father, Henry IV, to ward off domestic uprisings by encouraging "foreign quarrels," the prince took to heart this counsel: shortly after his father's death, the new monarch contemplated invading France.

Before undertaking his plans for war, young Henry inquired of the Archbishop of Canterbury as to whether he thought that an English monarch might "with right and conscience" lay claim to France. Having previously discussed with the Bishop of Ely how profitable such an invasion would be for the church, the Archbishop urged Henry to "invoke the warlike spirit" of his ancestors, who had brought "defeat on the full power of France." After all, he assured the King, France belonged to Henry by ancient law; the French were merely preventing him from exercising his rightful rule over the country, "usurped from you and your progenitors."

… the Archbishop urged Henry to "invoke the warlike spirit" of his ancestors who had brought "defeat on the full power of France."

Ironically, their conversation was interrupted by French messengers sent by the imperious Dauphin, heir to the French throne. The messengers informed Henry that their prince would never allow the English to take possession of the French-governed dukedoms he had recently demanded:

> *Your highness, lately sending into France,*
> *Did claim some certain dukedoms in the right*
> *Of your great predecessor, King Edward the Third.*
> *In answer of which claim, the prince our master*
> *… bids you be advis'd: There's nought in France*
> *That can be with a nimble [dance] won.*

As a gesture of utter disdain, the Dauphin had sent Henry, as a "fun of treasure," tennis balls. This insulting reminder

Having been known as an irresponsible ne'er-do-well in his youth, Henry chose to manifest and consolidate his power on the battlefield.

of Henry's idle youth, however, only strengthened the youthful ruler's resolve "to strike [the Dauphin's] father's crown into the hazard." Henry vowed to make "many a thousand widows weep" in France. Having been known as an irresponsible ne'er-do-well in his youth, he would manifest and consolidate his power on the battlefield.

News of the planned invasion quickly spread. In the midst of preparing his troops, Henry was outraged to discover that the French had hired three Englishmen to murder him. He condemned the three traitors – who once had been his trusted companions – to death, and took his early detection of the murder plot as a sign that fate was on his side.

The French, meanwhile, debated the actual danger posed by Henry. Charles VI favored amassing "men of courage" to combat the English "with means defendant." His arrogant and incautious son, on the other hand, despised fearful displays of a country so "idly king'd" as England. Despite his countrymen's arguments to the contrary, the Dauphin persisted in thinking of Henry as no more than "a vain, giddy, shallow, humorous youth," wholly incapable of successfully waging war on France.

His sister, the Princess Katharine, however, was more pragmatic. Anticipating an English victory, she set out to learn as much English as she could, gaily reciting, "De fingres. De nayles, d' arms, d' ilbow ..."

Back in London, loyal Englishmen continued to respond to Henry's call to arms against France. Among them were a poor, wayward boy and a man named Pistol. Pistol had recently attended to the ailing Sir John Falstaff in the Boar's Head Tavern. Falstaff had once been the British Crown Prince's drinking companion in the days before his ascension to the throne. But after gaining the crown, Henry had denounced the old man, the rumor went, "killing his heart." Following Falstaff's death, Pistol had concluded that "men's faiths" were as fragile as "wafer cakes," and determined to enlist in the King's army "to suck" the spoils of war from France.

Accompanied by the young boy and some unscrupulous companions, Pistol joined the King's army. After they followed the King to Agincourt, however, Pistol and his cronies soon found themselves in a predicament. The King hung two of Pistol's friends for "filching" goods

… the French king sent his messenger, Mountjoy, to Henry to apprise him that his troops were of "too faint a number" to win all of France.

from French citizens and, before long, cowardly Pistol fled the battlefield. Only the wayward boy remained, to "seek some better service" for his King.

Henry's resolve soon surprised and impressed even his staunchest detractors. Rejecting Charles's peace offering of "Katharine his daughter" and a dowry of "some petty and unprofitable dukedoms," Henry seized the city of Harfleur, which fell easily to the English; the fortifications the Dauphin had promised had never materialized. Nevertheless, the French king sent his messenger, Mountjoy, to Henry to apprise him that his troops were of "too faint a number" to win all of France. Furthermore, Charles demanded a "ransom" and an act of contrition: he wanted to see the British monarch kneeling in deference to the French throne.

"Thou dost thy office fairly," Henry told Mountjoy. "My people are with sickness much enfeebled." Still, Henry refused to give in to Charles's demands. His message to the French king was unwavering: "Yet, God before, tell him we will come on.…"

Determined to press on to victory, Henry realized that he must first embolden his "weak and sickly guard." Thus, disguised as a Welshman in an old cloak "walking from watch to watch, from tent to tent," he wandered about the camp, speaking of "fierceness," "obedience" and "conscience" to his unsuspecting soldiers. Unaware that they were in the presence of their monarch, the men listened as the cloaked stranger affirmed that the king's cause was "just and his quarrel honorable."

Inwardly, though, Henry harbored doubts about the justice of his cause. Was it worth the lives of his loyal subjects? "Every subject's duty is the King's," he reasoned, "but every subject's soul is his own." Bearing the responsibility of the lives of men was a "hard condition," he ruminated. "What infinite heart's ease must kings neglect, that private men enjoy!"

By daybreak, however, Henry roused his soldiers with a powerful call to arms. "This day is call'd the feast of Crispian," he began. "He that outlives this day and comes safe home will stand a-tiptoe when this day is named." Each man would forever mark and would celebrate Saint Crispian's day:

> Old men forget; yet all shall be forgot,
> But he'll remember with advantages
> What feats he did that day. Then shall our names,
> Familiar in his mouth as household words –
> Henry the King, Bedford and Exeter,
> Warwick and Talbot, Salisbury and Gloucester –
> Be in their flowing cups freshly remember'd.

The troops took their monarch's words to heart and battled for victory. Despite their meager numbers, they fought courageously on the fields of Agincourt. In the decisive moment of the conflict, Henry, grieving for the loss of two of his companions, ordered that "every soldier kill his prisoners" – an action that, ultimately, greatly strengthened the British position, giving Henry's army the battle.

Once again Mountjoy appeared and acknowledged England's victory: "The day is yours," he conceded. Then, with deference, he asked Henry's permission to bury the multitudes of French dead who lay on the fields. Now Henry gloated, exulting that "ten thousand French" had died in the Battle of Agincourt while, miraculously, the English had lost fewer than thirty. Among those killed was

"Every subject's duty is the King's," he reasoned, "but every subject's soul is his own."

the boy who had come to France with Pistol. Henry immediately called for the "holy rites" of funeral to be bestowed on the English dead.

Henry then set off for Charles's palace. When he arrived, he addressed the French king and his court magnanimously: "Peace to this meeting, wherefore we are met." He then proposed a truce, providing Charles would agree to England's demands. Sending his councilors off to attend to the particulars of the agreement, Henry announced that Katharine was his "capital demand" and that he wished to meet with her alone.

"O fair Katharine, if you will love me soundly with your French heart," Henry told the beautiful French princess after the others had left the room, "I will be glad to hear you confess it brokenly with your English tongue."

After contemplating her position and admitting that she did indeed feel something for him, the princess wondered aloud, "Is it possible dat I should love de enemy of France?" But Henry, as skilled in the art of persuasion as in war, assured his bride-to-be that in loving him he would henceforth be "the friend of France."

COMMENTARY

Probably written in 1599, *The Life of Henry V* was not an unqualified success. While one Elizabethan document noted that *Henry* "hath been sundry play'd," following a performance for the court of King James, the 17th-century critics largely ignored the play.

Henry V did not attract much critical attention until the early part of the 18th century, and even then the reviews were mixed. In 1817, for instance, the critic William Hazlitt wrote that Shakespeare's Henry "was a hero," but only in the sense that "he was ready to sacrifice his own life for the pleasure of destroying thousands of other lives." Hazlitt went on to call the play's protagonist "a very amiable monster" who only served to evoke the audience's "romantic, heroic, patriotic and poetical delight" in the King's daring-do. For Hazlitt, Shakespeare's *Henry V* epitomized the awful results of brutality and immorality.

As numerous later critics have noted, however, the play is about war. The historical Henry, more warlord than statesman, proved to be at his best when manifesting his unflinching patriotic zeal on the battlefield. In large measure, Shakespeare used the brutality of war to create a dramatic context in which to develop his Henry character. Were it not for Henry's singular responsibility for the bloodshed, the play would be devoid of drama. In the playwright's hands, Henry is a paradox, composed equally of recklessness and youthful exuberance, rooted in both love of self and love of country. Amid the heroic glory, carefree individualism and patriotic duty portrayed by Henry, Shakespeare vividly illustrates how much is sacrificed in the quest for greatness.

"Is it possible dat
I should love de
enemy of France?"

Henry VIII

TYPE OF WORK

Political drama

SETTING

London, England;
Sixteenth century

PRINCIPAL CHARACTERS

Henry VIII
Tudor King of England

Katharine of Aragon
Queen of England

Anne Bullen
Henry's lover and subsequent queen

Wolsey
Ambitious Cardinal of York

Duke Buckingham
Wolsey's adversary

**Duke of Norfolk and
Duke of Suffolk**
Also Wolsey's enemies

Cranmer
Archbishop of Canterbury

Two noblemen, the Dukes Norfolk and Buckingham, met in the palace to converse. Norfolk was angered by the audacity of Henry VIII, who had signed a peace treaty with Francis I of France – a treaty financed by Cardinal Wolsey of York. Norfolk warned his friend of Wolsey's equal hatred for Buckingham: "Like it, your Grace, the state takes notice of the private difference betwixt you and the cardinal. I advise you … that you read the cardinal's malice and his potency together; to consider further that what his high hatred would effect wants not a minister in his power."

Just then Wolsey entered the palace and, after exchanging disdainful glances with Buckingham, headed towards the king's chamber. "I read in's looks matter against me," Buckingham whispered. "And his eye reviled me as his abject object…. He's gone to th' king!" Taking note of Buckingham's alarm and anger, Norfolk advised him to act prudently. Still, shortly thereafter, Buckingham was arrested for treason.

Meanwhile, in the throne room, Queen Katharine chided her husband about the heavy tax burden that Wolsey had ostensibly levied on the

"I read in's looks matter against me," Buckingham whispered. "And his eye reviled me as his abject object…. He's gone to th' king!"

people. "Your subjects are in great grievance," she said, "and almost appear in loud rebellion." Unknown to King Henry, Norfolk had in actuality instituted a tax, in an effort to stir up Henry's subjects against the cardinal. Now the King demanded to know what she meant: "Taxation? Wherein? and what taxation? My lord Cardinal … know you of this taxation?" When Wolsey denied any knowledge of the affair, Henry immediately had the collections stopped.

Now Henry, in the same way that he was accustomed to executing slanderous dukes, was prone also to divorcing his wives.

Katharine later inquired about the Duke of Buckingham. Why had he been arrested? Henry and Wolsey brought forth their witness to Buckingham's treason. This man claimed to have heard Buckingham say, in effect, that if the King should die without male posterity then he would make the throne his own. Wolsey also stepped forward and further testified that Buckingham had suggested he would go so far as to kill his sovereign in order to gain the scepter. Henry was convinced: "By day and night, he's traitor to the height."

That week at a party given by Cardinal Wolsey, Henry met Anne Bullen. He was taken by her beauty and impulsively kissed her. And, on the following day, Henry sent Lord Chamberlain to bestow upon Anne the title of "Marchioness of Pembroke; to which … a thousand pounds a year, annual support, out of his grace he adds." Hours later, Buckingham was declared guilty of treason and condemned to die.

Now Henry, in the same way that he was accustomed to executing slanderous dukes, was prone also to divorcing his wives. With King Henry's infatuation with Anne, prompt separation from Queen Katharine was inevitable.

A court of divorce was convened, in which Katherine, kneeling at her husband's feet, pled her case:

… Alas, sir,
In what have I offended you?…
Heaven witness,
I have been to you a true and humble wife,
At all times to your will conformable.…
When was the hour
I ever contradicted your desire,
Or made it not mine too?…

Katherine, kneeling at Henry's feet, pled her case: "Alas, sir, in what have I offended you?… I have been to you a true and humble wife, at all times to your will conformable …"

"I have touched the highest point of all my greatness, and from that full meridian of my glory I haste now to my setting."

Then the Queen directed her ire toward Wolsey: "I do believe … that you are mine enemy; [but] you shall not be my judge." But the deceitful cardinal refused to step down from the judge's seat, and Katharine, realizing that she had already lost her cause to Henry's whims, retired.

"The queen of earthly queens," Henry lamented at her departure. Nevertheless, addressing the court, he stated his reasons for petitioning for divorce: his wife had not produced a male heir, and "I weighed the danger which my realms stood in by this my issue's fail.…" But one of his advisors cautioned him that Katharine had likely gone to appeal her case to the pope. To this potential challenge, the king replied, "I abhor this dilatory sloth and tricks of Rome."

Soon, Katharine was visited by Wolsey and another cardinal in an attitude of friendship and reconciliation, but she was not duped. "… Ye wish for my ruin," she charged, vowing to fight them and to restore herself to her former place of dignity, or die.

Back at the king's court, Norfolk, Suffolk, Surrey and Chamberlain all warily watched the cardinal's rapid rise to power. Chamberlain warned the others of Wolsey's influence over Henry: "I much fear. If you cannot bar his access to th' king, never attempt anything on him; for he hath a witchcraft over th' king's tongue." Suffolk, though, was unafraid. He knew that the letters the cardinal had sent to the pope had "miscarried and came to th' eye o' the king." These letters, intercepted by Henry, disclosed Wolsey's disloyalty. They urged the pope to stay the divorce because the King was "tangled in affection to … Lady Anne Bullen." King Henry hid his ire at this, Wolsey's devious act, and promptly married Anne, in defiance of the church.

Days later, at the castle, Henry sought out Wolsey. "What piles of wealth hath he accumulated to his own portion …" he stormed. "It may well be, there is a mutiny in's mind." Finally finding the cardinal, the King laid out the self-written evidence convicting him of disloyalty. As Wolsey looked over his own letters, filled with defamation toward his monarch, he cried, "I have touched the highest point of all my greatness, and from that full meridian of my glory I haste now to my setting."

King Henry hid his ire at this, Wolsey's devious act, and immediately married Anne, in defiance of the church.

The other nobles exulted in Wolsey's misfortune. Surrey gloated openly to Wolsey: "Thy ambition thou scarlet sin, robb'd this bewailing land …" and Suffolk also chimed in: "The king's further pleasure is … that therefore such a writ be su'd against you, to forfeit all your goods, lands, tenements, chattels, and whatsoever., and to be out of the king's protection.…" Then, their verbal barrage ended, the noblemen left the broken cardinal in his misery. As he bewailed his "fallen" state, Cromwell entered and informed him that Sir Thomas More had just been chosen Lord Chancellor in his place. "Farewell the hopes of court; my hopes in heaven do dwell," Wolsey cried.

That same day, the coronation of Queen Anne Bullen was celebrated amid much pomp and splendor.

Now living in exile, Katharine discussed the recent news from London with her gentleman usher, Griffith. Griffith told her that Wolsey had taken ill as he was being transported to the tower of London after his arrest, and had died "full of repentance, continued meditations, tears and sorrows; he gave his honors to the world again … and slept in peace." Saddened, Katharine fell asleep herself, and as she slumbered, beheld a vision of six personages clad in white robes, who "promised me eternal happiness and brought me garlands," as she told Griffith when she awoke. Griffith, noticing how weak and pale the woman appeared, he sobbed, "She is going."

Soon, a messenger arrived from King Henry expressing his grief over Katharine's illness. "… That comfort comes too late," the former queen replied. "'Tis like a pardon after execution." She then asked the messenger:

Remember me
In all humility unto his highness:
Say his long trouble now is passing

"Remember me in all humility unto his highness: Say, his long trouble now is passing out of this world; tell him, in death, I blessed him.… I was a chaste wife to my grave …"

Out of this world. Tell him,
in death I bless'd him....
I was a chaste wife to my grave.

Archbishop Cranmer pronounced that "this royal infant ... though still in her cradle, yet now promises upon this land a thousand thousand blessings."

Some time later, it was whispered in court that Queen Anne was in labor with child and "that her suff'rance made almost pang a death." An old sorceress visited the king to report Anne's labors. Henry begged the woman to tell him that he had a son, but she brought other tidings. "'Tis a girl," she told him. Nevertheless, before she departed she promised him a future male heir.

While Henry went to see his wife and newborn child, his councilors held an assembly in secret. Their intent was to seize power by imprisoning the Archbishop of Canterbury, Cranmer, for "heresies." But just then the King unexpectedly entered the chamber and prevented the arrest. After reprimanding the nobles for their disrespect toward the Archbishop, he turned to Cranmer and humbly asked, "Lord of Canterbury, I have a suit which you must not deny me; that is, a fair young maid that yet wants baptism, you must be godfather and answer for her."

Again royalty gathered in grandeur, with trumpets blaring, to witness the baptism of Henry's daughter, Elizabeth. Archbishop Cranmer pronounced that "this royal infant ... though still in her cradle, yet now promises upon this land a thousand thousand blessings." He further prophesied that Elizabeth "shall be, to the happiness of England, an aged princess ... but she must die ... yet a virgin, a most unspotted lily shall she pass to the ground, and all the world shall mourn her."

King Henry smiled: "This oracle of comfort has so pleas'd me, that when I am in heaven, I shall desire to see what this child does...."

COMMENTARY

From the start, this play seemed scourged. It closed after its debut because a fire burned down the theater where it was being performed. Critics have lambasted *Henry VIII* for its lack of action and rather anticlimactic ending. But the play was designed more as a display piece for its rich and elaborate staging and costumes than for its action or intrigue.

Another criticism leveled at the drama was its avoidance of the issues of the Protestant Reformation in England. Shakespeare was careful not to imply that the events of the play – Henry's divorce of Katharine and his subsequent marriage to Anne – had led in any way to England's still smoldering break with the Church in Rome. By limiting himself to a more subdued plot, Shakespeare tactfully avoided insulting the ruling House of Tudor. On the other hand, the drama does explore the type of political intrigue that may have actually taken place in the court of this flamboyant and controversial monarch.

Richard II

TYPE OF WORK

Political-intrigue tragedy

SETTING

Fourteenth century
England and Wales

PRINCIPAL CHARACTERS

Richard II
King of England

Queen Isabel
Richard's wife

Henry Bolingbroke
*His cousin (who later becomes
King Henry IV)*

Thomas Mowbray
*Bolingbroke's enemy,
Duke of Norfolk*

**The Earl of
Northumberland**
One of Bolingbroke's supporters

Duke of Aumerle
*Another of Richard's cousins,
and a supporter*

John of Gaunt
*Richard's uncle, and Bolingbroke's
father*

The Duke of York
*Another of Richard's uncles, and
Aumerle's father*

Early in his rule, Richard II had arranged for the murder
of one of his uncles, the Duke of Gloucester – although
it was not widely known that he had ordered the uncle's
death. Richard II's cousin, Bolingbroke, instead blamed
a man named Thomas Mowbray for planning the murder
of the Duke and for swindling money from the military.
Denouncing Bolingbroke as a liar, Mowbray vehemently
denied these accusations.

The dispute between the two men had grown so
ugly that King Richard found it necessary to intercede.
Commanding Bolingbroke and Mowbray to appear before
him, he listened to their venomous exchange – and soon
concluded that there was no recourse but to let "swords
and lances" settle their grievances.

On the day Richard had appointed for the duel, he
and his court assembled at Coventry. But combat was
not in the cards. Richard surprised the crowd by declaring
that such a rivalry could only lead to civil war. Instead of
jousting, both men would be "banished," he declared –
Bolingbroke for six years, Mowbray forever. "A heavy
sentence," Bolingbroke despaired; and Mowbray,
despondent, said that he would henceforth "dwell in
solemn shades of endless night." After warning the King
to be wary of the lying Bolingbroke, Mowbray sorrowfully
disappeared, and Bolingbroke prepared for his own
departure. Before he went, however, he swore that

wherever he might roam he would always boast that he was indeed "a true-born Englishman."

Not long after Bolingbroke left England, Richard relaxed at court with friends and another cousin, the Duke Aumerle. "What said our cousin when you parted with him?" Richard asked Aumerle. "'Farewell,'" Aumerle joked. Then Aumerle informed the King that he in fact felt nothing but disdain for Bolingbroke. Scorning his banished cousin as well, Richard poked fun at Bolingbroke's popular appeal:

[Observe] his courtship to the common people;
How he did seem to dive into their hearts
With humble and familiar courtesy;
What reverence he did throw away on slaves....

… invoking the privilege of a dying man, Gaunt chastised the King for his royal extravagance that had nearly bankrupt England …

One of Richard's friends then changed the subject; there was a much more pressing issue the King needed to confront: a rebellion in Ireland. "We will make for Ireland presently," Richard agreed. But, he wondered, how could he finance the journey? At that very moment he received news that would provide him with the answer: his uncle Gaunt, the Duke of Lancaster – and the exiled Bolingbroke's father – was "grievous sick" and on the verge of death. This uncle's "coffers" would outfit soldiers for the Irish wars, thought Richard.

> There was a much more pressing issue the King needed to confront: a rebellion in Ireland.

Waiting for Richard to arrive at his side, the ailing Gaunt was attended by his brother the Duke of York. "Methinks I am a prophet new inspired," the dying man said, lamenting the divisions within his beloved England. Although York advised his brother not to waste his breath counseling their nephew Richard, Gaunt would not listen. And when Richard arrived, invoking the privilege of a dying man, Gaunt chastised the King for his royal extravagance that had nearly bankrupt England, and for the "flatterers" at court. Furious, Richard struck back at Gaunt as a "lunatic, lean-witted fool."

Shortly thereafter, Richard's uncle died. The King then revealed the true nature of his visit to Gaunt's house: to demand all the "plate, coin, revenues, and movables" of his estate. Horrified by Richard's callousness and greed, York pleaded with his nephew the King not to cause any more dissension within the family. But Richard dismissed his uncle's words; he was in need of Gaunt's estate to back his wars with the Irish. Then he added that he expected

York to govern England while he was away. Before his nephew departed, York warned him that he would suffer for his selfishness, that "bad courses" could never "fall out good."

"Comfort's in heaven, and we are on the earth …"

York's words proved prophetic. With Richard away in Ireland in company of Aumerle and others of his entourage, York soon found himself in the midst of a precarious situation: outraged by Richard's seizure of his father's estate, Bolingbroke had broken his exile, returned to England, and amassed a force of insurrectionists to retrieve it. Richard's wife was quite shaken by this news. "Uncle, for God's sake, speak comfortable words," she begged York. But York could not offer the Queen solace. "Comfort's in heaven, and we are on the earth," he regretfully sighed.

Not long afterwards, York set off to meet Bolingbroke in Gloucestershire, where his nephew had made camp. Though angered by what had happened, Bolingbroke felt no animosity towards York; he welcomed him warmly, calling him "gracious uncle."

York, on the other hand, did not regard his nephew entirely amiably; he reprimanded him, "Tut, tut! Grace me no grace, nor uncle me no uncle." Reminding his nephew that he had been banished by the "anointed king," York denounced Bolingbroke for his "gross rebellion and detested treason."

One of Bolingbroke's supporters, the Earl of Northumberland, intervened to plead with York. Could he not see that his nephew had been much abused by the King? Seeing some truth in these words, York began to relent. Still, his loyalties were divided between his two nephews. "I am neutral," York finally stated firmly. But no sooner had he uttered these words than he seemed to align himself with Bolingbroke, offering him and his rebels both "shelter" and "repose" in a nearby castle.

A short while later, Richard left Ireland and arrived at Wales, delighted to be once more in his kingdom. He had learned of his cousin's insurrection, but he was not greatly concerned: Richard felt certain that "all the water in the rough rude sea" could not depose an "anointed king." However, his confidence was soon shaken when he heard that York's Welsh troops – who had promised to support the monarchy – had gone over to Bolingbroke. Richard became despondent at the news. "Comfort, my liege, remember who you are," Aumerle encouraged his cousin. Nonetheless, even as Richard's mood started to brighten, he was brought news just as disturbing: Bolingbroke had beheaded several of Richard's closest courtiers, and still the man's influence among the commoners and royalty alike continued to grow. Richard despaired:

Our lands, our lives, and all are Bolingbroke's,
And nothing can we call our own but death
And that small model of the barren earth
Which serves as paste and cover to our bones.

Richard felt certain that "all the water in the rough rude sea" could not depose an "anointed king."

Now destitute of both friendship and power, Richard sought refuge at Flint Castle, where, he reckoned, he would simply "pine away." Troubled by the King's lack of confidence, Aumerle tried mightily to restore his spirits. But Richard would not listen to his cousin, warning him that "flatteries" did harm.

When Bolingbroke discovered that Richard had gone to Flint Castle, he sent the Earl of Northumberland there with word that Bolingbroke on "both his knees doth kiss King Richard's hand." But Northumberland did not kneel. Observing this offense, Richard – from a platform high on the castle – called down to Northumberland, berating him, "How dare thy joints forget" to show "duty to our presence?" The wily and cruel Northumberland did not respond to the King's admonishment, but merely informed Richard that Bolingbroke only wanted to reclaim his rights, his "lineal royalties." If these rights were restored and his banishment overturned, Bolingbroke's insurrection would end. At once, Richard decreed that Bolingbroke's demands would "be accomplished without contradictions."

"How dare thy joints forget" to show "duty to our presence?"

Our hands,
our lives,
and all are
Bolingbroke's,
And nothing
can we call
our own but
death ...

A moment later, however, Richard had misgivings. Turning to Aumerle, he wondered if he had not been too quick to "debase" himself. But just then Bolingbroke himself arrived, and Richard went down to the courtyard to meet his cousin. Seeing his rival kneel before him, Richard chided, "Fair cousin, you debase your princely knee." Only then did Richard suddenly perceive that he had been tricked by Northumberland: Bolingbroke intended to steal his throne. "What you will have, I'll give, and willing too," Richard pled, but it was too late. Bolingbroke and his followers seized Richard and spirited him back to London.

Although he was forced to hand his crown over to his cousin, Richard wavered. True, he had no choice in the matter, but who would he be if not the King? "I must nothing be," he mourned. Utterly defeated, Richard cried that he had nothing, not even the name he had received "at the font." Finally, Bolingbroke, now the proclaimed

Horrified, York denounced his son and rushed to the castle to warn his new King of the murderous plan.

King Henry IV, informed him that he was to be imprisoned in the Tower of London.

As Richard was being led to prison, Northumberland arrived to inform the deposed king that he was to be imprisoned in Pomfret Castle, instead of the Tower, and that his wife "must away to France." In agony, the former Queen begged Northumberland,

Utterly defeated, Richard cried that he had nothing, not even the name he had received "at the font."

"Banish us both, and send the King with me." But Northumberland ignored her. "One more adieu," Richard told his distraught wife as he was led toward Pomfret Castle, "the rest let sorrow say."

"Alack, poor Richard!" York's wife lamented when she heard of his fate at Bolingbroke's hands. But her husband cautioned her that they all now had to pledge "lasting fealty to the new-made king." Moments later, however, their son Aumerle returned home and confessed of a plan that much alarmed his parents: he was part of a plot to murder Bolingbroke. Horrified, York denounced his son and rushed to the castle to warn his new King of the murderous plan, the Duchess and Aumerle following behind. Arriving at the castle, the Duchess begged, "Forever will I walk upon my knees," if only the King would forgive her son and spare his life. Henry IV astonished them all. "I will pardon him," he readily agreed, "as God shall pardon me." But, he informed them, the other conspirators would "not live within this world."

Soon afterward, the new monarch, uneasy in the thought that Richard could yet be restored to the throne, decided that the prisoner would have to die. Meanwhile, unaware of this edict, Richard agonized in his solitude at

Pomfret Castle, passing the long hours questioning the nature of his own existence. Was he a "king"? Or was he a "beggar"? Or was he simply "nothing" at all? At last he concluded, "I wasted time, and now doth Time waste me."

One day when his jail-keeper brought his meal, Richard asked him to taste the food as the keeper was "wont to do." The keeper refused. Right off suspecting treachery, Richard attacked the man, who screamed – which was all according to the new monarch's plan. Suddenly, hired murderers dashed into the room. Outwitting them, Richard wrested away one attacker's weapon and killed him. Then he felled another. But a third knight, the faithful Sir Exton, Henry's principal schemer in the assassination plot, overtook Richard and delivered a mortal blow. Falling, Richard cried, "The king's blood stained the king's own land."

When Sir Exton returned with Richard's body, Henry banished the killer forever to hide his own treachery.

Proclaiming hatred for the "murderer," Henry insisted that he loved his poor dead cousin, and vowed to make a pilgrimage to the Holy Land – an atoning pilgrimage that, he hoped, would "wash this blood from my guilty hand."

Falling, Richard cried, "the king's blood stained the king's own land."

COMMENTARY

*R*ichard II was one of Shakespeare's most popular plays. In his time, he may have intended audiences to feel sympathy for Richard, since he believed his position to be "anointed" by God Himself. On the contrary, Bolingbroke may evoke more sympathy from a contemporary audience, since his character reflects a will of the people.

Shakespeare's greatest strength was his ability to accurately portray on stage the turbulent, sometimes lethal, events that shaped English history. In Richard, he succeeds masterfully.

Richard III

TYPE OF WORK

Political drama

SETTING

Fifteenth century England
(London, Salisbury
and Bosworth Field)

PRINCIPAL CHARACTERS

Richard
*Duke of Gloucester, a treacherous,
jealous, murderous aristocrat, and
brother of King Edward IV*

King Edward IV
*King of England, Richard's elder
brother*

George
*Duke of Clarence, Richard's and
Edward's youngest brother*

Queen Elizabeth
Edward's wife

The Duchess of York
*Mother to Richard, George and
King Edward*

Duke of Buckingham
A cousin to Richard

Queen Margaret
*Widow of King Henry VI,
who was killed by Richard*

Lady Anne
*A widow whose husband and
father-in-law were also killed by
Richard*

For having defeated them in battle – and to win back the
throne – the sons of Richard II sought retribution against
the family of Henry VI. Richard III, the most brutal
of three brothers, murdered Henry's ailing son, stabbing
him while the Queen looked on. Cursing them all, the
Queen singled out the hunchbacked Richard III, calling
him "the devil's butcher." In a frothing rage, young
Richard sought out the king, whom he murdered on the
spot. Richard's eldest brother, Edward, was then declared
King of England. The stage for what was to come "had
now been set."

Richard III stood on the streets of London,
gloating about the victorious House of York. Though he
had been instrumental in helping his brother to the throne,
he now aspired for it himself. But his thoughts soon turned
to his own deformity:

> *Cheated of feature by dissembling nature,*
> *Deform'd, unfinished, sent before my time*
> *Into this breathing world, scarce half made up …*

Richard then took consolation in his own cleverness.
In fact, he had just succeeded in pitting his brothers, King
Edward and Clarence, against each other: He had tricked
the King into believing there was a prophecy in which
a kinsman, whose name began with the letter "G," would

murder the King and win the throne. In response, King
Edward had his brother, Clarence – whose given name was
George – arrested.

In the midst of Richard's meditations, Clarence passed
by, accompanied by an armed guard taking him to the
Tower of London. Richard pretended to be shocked and
outraged, and hinted that the King's wife or his mistress
was responsible for Clarence's arrest. As soon as Clarence
was out of sight, however, Richard, as deceitful in word as
in deed, vowed to kill him, formulating how, for Richard's
own political gain.

With the same thoughts for his brother Edward,
Richard devised how God could, for Richard's own
political gain, "take King Edward to his mercy." Besides the
power it would bring, a position near – or on – the throne
would make him a more attractive suitor for Lady Anne,
one of the last remaining members of the once-powerful
House of Lancaster – even though Richard had killed both
her husband and her father-in-law.

> ... a position
> near – or on – the
> throne would
> make him a more
> attractive suitor
> for Lady Anne.

A short while later, Richard spied Lady Anne as she followed the casket of her father-in-law, Henry VI, all the while cursing the treacherous Duke for his crimes. When he approached, she lashed out at him, spewing, "thou dreadful minister of hell."

Though he had been instrumental in helping his brother to the throne, he now aspired it for himself.

But in an effort to deceive her, Richard hastily proclaimed his love for her, claiming that he had murdered her husband and father-in-law only to win for himself her "heavenly face." Feigning guilt, he even pronounced that he would lend her his "sharp-pointed sword" to kill him so that she might avenge the deaths. Not only did she refuse, she eventually agreed to wear Richard's ring. And before she departed, the foolish Anne told him how happy she was that he had "become so penitent."

Richard then decided to go to the palace to create trouble for Queen Elizabeth – Edward's wife – and her kinsmen. "A plague upon you all," he cried, accusing them in mock anger of imprisoning his brother Clarence. Meanwhile, the former Queen, Margaret – Lady Anne's mother-in-law – entered, muttering to herself her loathing for Richard, the slayer of her husband and son. But Margaret finally could no longer bear to seethe quietly; she came forward and denounced all of them as "wrangling pirates" who had stolen her sovereignty. "Foul wrinkled witch," Richard hissed back at her. Thoroughly maddened by this insult, she cursed the House of York and predicted that Richard would bring ruin to all of them:

O! but remember this another day,
When he shall split thy very heart with sorrow,

Richard then proclaimed his love for her – he had murdered her husband and father-in-law only to win for himself her "heavenly face."

And say poor Margaret was a prophetess.
Live each of you the subjects to his hate,
And he to yours, and all of you to God's!

Not long after, Richard met with two assassins, whom he hired to murder his brother Clarence. He instructed them to do the deed quickly, then sent them off.

When these two reached the Tower prison, they found Clarence sleeping. Earlier, he had complained to his keeper about "fearful dreams of drowning." As if in fulfillment of prophecy, the assassins, after much arguing about the advisability of killing Clarence, first stabbed him, then immersed him in a cask of wine.

In the meantime, the gravely ill King Edward had called his own and his wife's families – including Richard – to his side and begged them to be "peaceful." Queen Elizabeth persuaded the King to pardon Clarence. But immediately Richard exclaimed, "But he, poor man, by your first order died." Edward grieved terribly at this news – little suspecting that Richard had been responsible for the death. Then Richard took his cousin, Buckingham, aside, and remarked how "guilty" of Clarence's execution the Queen's kinsmen appeared.

Richard met with two assassins, whom he hired to murder his brother Clarence.

Fearing for the safety of her grandchildren, next in line for the throne, Edward's – and Richard's – mother, the Duchess of York, arranged to take Edward's sons to a sanctuary. Richard, however, persuaded the princes to go to the Tower, where, he said, they would be safer. Reluctantly, the princes did as he bade. They thought their grandmother and mother would join them later after arranging the coronation, but, alas, the youngsters would not again see the light of day.

Still, Richard was not satisfied. Having not yet gained public support, he conspired with Buckingham to spread lies about the legitimacy of the late King Edward. When the English citizenry rejected these rumors, Richard planned to feign reluctance to accept the throne. On the day of his coronation, he would stand between two priests with a prayer book in his hand.

Once everyone had been assembled according to plan, Buckingham begged Richard to take control of the "kingly government." Richard declined, pretending to be a faithful supporter of the Crown Prince – who, for his "safety," was

… his dreams were haunted by the voices of his victims, who cheered on the Earl of Richmond.

locked up in the Tower. The scheme worked so well that before long the Mayor of London appealed to Richard, "Do, good my lord; the citizens entreat you." With false humility, Richard agreed to be king. And then with one last deception, he added, "Albeit against my conscience and my soul."

So, with Buckingham's help, he was crowned King Richard III. Buckingham, however, soon fell out of Richard's favor. One day referring to the young princes, Richard snarled, "I want the bastards dead." When Buckingham balked at the order, Richard became enraged – and quickly hired an assassin to smother the little princes in their sleep.

Word was soon sent to Anne that Richard demanded that she become his Queen. Filled with trepidation, Anne went.

Not long after the princes were murdered, Richard decided also to kill his new wife, Anne. After the deed was done, he proclaimed that she had died of an illness – so that he could then pursue the beautiful Princess Elizabeth, Edward's daughter.

Queen Elizabeth, who still did not know the fate of her sons, was outraged when she learned of Richard's intentions to marry her daughter, and claimed she would corrupt the young girl before she would let her marry Richard. But he was unfazed. So Elizabeth said she would consult with her daughter and return with her decision.

Soon, the tide of fate gathered against Richard. Word was brought that the Earl of Richmond, a suitor of the throne, had gathered a naval fleet off the coast of Milford. At the Earl's side was Buckingham, Richard's defected accomplice. Another messenger brought news that revolts had sprung up in the realm, which angered Richard.

He struck the man and told him to bring better news next time. And, in fact, a third messenger did convey better news: Buckingham had been captured in Salisbury and was asking to see Richard. Denying the request, the King ordered the execution of his old friend. "Wrong hath but wrong," he mused, penitently, "and blame the due of blame."

Soon, Richard made his way to Bosworth Field, where his forces would meet the Earl's. Settled into his tent the night before the battle, he found himself more downhearted than usual. Finally, he fell asleep, but his dreams were haunted by the voices of his victims, who cheered on the Earl of Richmond.

The next day, Richard led his soldiers into battle. Before meeting his foe, Richard's horse was killed. As Richard frantically searched the field for a mount, crying out, "A horse! My kingdom for a horse!" the Earl of Richmond fell upon him and killed him. The Earl then proclaimed his intentions to marry Princess Elizabeth, and to put the long war between the House of York and the House of Lancaster to rest. England would know peace at last.

COMMENTARY

This final work in the Bard's series of historical plays is quite devoid of typical prose and song. Chronologically, King Richard III was the last English sovereign of the House of York, whose death in 1483 led to the establishment – by Henry, Duke of Richmond – of today's Tudor monarchy. Richard III the monarch has been viewed more favorably by historians than by Shakespeare:

he apparently was no more – or less – treacherous than others of his lineage.

Shakespeare created an unusually powerful, dramatic persona in the character of Richard, imbuing him with such a heinous nature that other characters in the tragedy refer to him, time and time again, as a "devil." His own mother eventually bewails her "accursed womb" for giving him life; and Richard himself confesses, "Alas, I rather hate myself…. I am a villain."

In spite of his evil nature, Richard evokes surprising sympathy, perhaps due to his evolution – or devolution – from monster to mere mortal.

"A horse! My kingdom for a horse!"

SCARAB

ORDER INFORMATION

This book makes the perfect gift.
To order this or other fine Scarab products, visit our website:

www.scarabbooks.com

Graffiti